Preaching Romans

Proclaiming God's Saving Grace

Frank J. Matera

LITURGICAL PRESS
Collegeville, Minnesota

www.litpress.org

Cover design by David Manahan, OSB. Cover illustration: *Saint Paul Writing His Epistles*, painting by Valentin de Boulogne, 1591–1632. Courtesy of the Sarah Campbell Blaffer Foundation, Houston, Texas.

1   2   3   4   5   6   7   8   9

Library of Congress Cataloging-in-Publication Data

Matera, Frank J.
   Preaching Romans : proclaiming God's saving grace / Frank J. Matera.
     p. cm.
   ISBN 978-0-8146-3318-2 – ISBN 978-0-8146-3913-9 (e-book)
    1. Bible. N.T. Romans–Homiletical use.   2. Catholic preaching.
  3. Bible. N.T. Romans–Sermons.   4. Sermons, American–21st
century.   5. Catholic Church–Sermons.   I. Title.

   BS2665.54.M38 2010
   227'.107–dc22   2009045835

"Homilists who have avoided preaching Paul's powerful but daunting Letter to the Romans needn't shirk their duty any longer. Matera's book does it all—biblical exposition, sample homilies with post-delivery analysis, and explicit strategies for preparing homilies. This is a rare and valuable pastoral resource written by one of the best contemporary Catholic interpreters of Paul. A 'must have' reference for preachers! Also valuable for *anyone* wanting to know more about Romans and its message for today."

> — Ronald D. Witherup, SS
> Author of *Biblical Fundamentalism:*
> *What Every Catholic Should Know* (Liturgical Press)

"Once again, Fr. Matera proves that he should be ranked among our best guides for preaching Paul. This small volume on Romans ingeniously outlines homiletic strategies for the liturgical year that are altogether lucid, well organized and pastoral. Matera's vast experience as both a biblical scholar and minister of the Word discloses itself on every page."

> — Guerric DeBona, OSB
> Professor of Homiletics
> Saint Meinrad Seminary and School of Theology

For the parishioners of Holy Family Parish,
Davidson, Maryland,
to whom I have been privileged to preach the gospel
of God's saving grace.

Contents

Acknowledgments

I acknowledge my gratitude to Baker Academic Press for permission to use material in part 1 ("Romans in Outline" and "A Synopsis of Romans") that comes from my forthcoming commentary, *Romans*, in the series Paideia (2010).

I am grateful to the National Pastoral Life Center for permission to use material in part 1 ("Themes for Preaching from Romans") that I first published in *Church* 18 (2002) 50–53.

Preaching from Romans

The Reason for This Book

Some years ago I wrote a small volume titled *Strategies for Preaching Paul* (Liturgical Press, 2001) in which I presented a method and rationale for preaching from the Pauline epistles. The purpose of that book was to provide homilists with a way to renew their preaching by making use of the Pauline texts of the Sunday Lectionary, thereby breaking the silence about the Pauline gospel that characterizes Catholic homiletics. Accordingly, I summarized the content and homiletical possibilities of the Pauline readings that occur in the Sunday Lectionary in order to introduce preachers to the rich theology of Paul's letters that can inform their preaching.

Since writing that book I have tried to practice what I urged others to do by preaching with some regularity from the Pauline texts. In doing so I have continued to uncover new themes that have enriched my own proclamation of the gospel. More importantly, I have learned to preach in what I call "a Pauline key." By this I mean that Pauline themes of redemption and sanctification, justification and reconciliation, resurrection and parousia now inform my preaching in ways they formerly did not, even when I am not preaching from Paul's letters. One of the great benefits of Pauline preaching, then, is that it invigorates and renews the whole of our preaching, since it opens our eyes to new and important ways of proclaiming the gospel.

During the summer of 2008 I decided to preach on a regular basis from Paul's letter to the Romans. There were three reasons for this. First, Year A of the Sunday Lectionary cycle occurred that particular year, dedicating sixteen consecutive weeks to Romans (this will occur again in 2011, 2014, 2017, etc). Second, the summer of 2008 marked the beginning of the Pauline Year, and I was already committed to presenting a series of workshops on preaching from Romans. Third, I was in the middle of writing a commentary on Romans that I have now completed (*Romans*, Baker Academic, 2010).

Preaching from Romans week after week proved to be a rewarding experience, since Romans is a powerful letter that focuses its attention on the saving righteousness of God. By committing myself to preaching from Romans over a four-month period, I sought to introduce the congregation to the Pauline gospel with its distinctive emphasis on the saving righteousness of God revealed in Jesus Christ.

Having preached from Romans and been enriched by the experience, I would like to share my experience in the hope that I might provide others with an incentive to preach from Paul and renew their own preaching. Accordingly, I have gathered in this volume the homilies that I preached on Romans. In doing so it is *not* my intent to present readers with a collection of my homilies. Rather, as is evident from the structure of this book, I have sought to explain *why* and *how* I preached these homilies as I did. In other words, my purpose is to talk about what it means to preach from Romans by showing and explaining how I preached from this great letter during the course of one summer.

Before each homily readers will find a brief section titled "Before the Homily" in which I explain the context of the text and the possibilities the text offers for preaching. Next, I reproduce the homily that I preached. In doing so I have highlighted the rhetorical techniques that I employed in order to persuade and engage the congregation. Finally, in a brief section titled "After the Homily," I analyze and explain my homily.

Since the Roman Lectionary also makes extensive use of Romans in the Weekday Lectionary of Year 1 (weeks 28–31), I have included a section on the weekday readings of Romans as well. But rather than present a series of homilies, I have summarized the central message of each reading with a view to highlighting what preachers might say in a brief homily of two or three minutes. These weekday selections from Romans are more extensive than those found in the Sunday Lectionary. Preachers who take advantage of studying and preaching from them will not only deepen their understanding of the Pauline gospel, they will also prepare themselves to preach from Romans when it occurs in the Sunday Lectionary.

Before turning to the texts of Romans, however, it will be helpful to explain my understanding of preaching and provide the readers of this volume with a brief overview of Romans and its central themes, the topics to which I now turn.

The Nature of Pauline Preaching

Although preaching is a public ministry intended to encourage and strengthen the believing community, it is also an art that differs from preacher to preacher. All preachers, for good or for ill, have a distinctive preaching style. Preachers tend to preach in the same way because they have developed habits and patterns for preparing and delivering their homilies.

Preachers can discover and analyze their preaching style by asking a few questions: How do I prepare to preach? How long are my homilies? Do I think out, outline, or write my homilies? What am I trying to achieve when I preach? What is the structure of my homily? What are my favorite rhetorical devices for persuading and encouraging the congregation?

Since I have been preaching for more than forty years, I too have developed patterns and habits for proclaiming the Word of God. A few years ago I analyzed my preaching and summarized my understanding of proclaiming God's Word. While I don't expect everyone to adopt my approach, before proceeding further the readers of this volume may find it helpful to understand how I preach. In this way they will know why they agree, or disagree, with me.

The Homily Is a Proclamation of Good News

The homily is not an exegetical lesson. Nor is it a sermon in the sense of an extended discourse or lecture. The homily is first and foremost an exposition and proclamation of the gospel. Those who preach the gospel are proclaiming good news: the good news that Jesus Christ brings about God, the good news of the in-breaking kingdom of God, the good news of what God has done in Jesus Christ, the good news of the new life that believers enjoy in their risen Lord. Accordingly, before they preach, homilists should ask themselves what is the good news they are bringing? Will those who listen to the homily leave with a renewed sense of purpose and meaning in their lives because they have heard the good news of Jesus Christ?

The Homily Belongs to the Rhetoric of Persuasion

Since the homilist is addressing a community of believers who have already committed themselves to the gospel, the homily belongs to the rhetoric of persuasion rather than to the rhetoric of teaching. It seeks to persuade believers to do what they already know they should do. Although most believers know, at some level, what they ought to do, they still need to be encouraged and persuaded to act in this way. This is why it is so important to hear the gospel and listen to the preached word again and again. The effective homilist, then, will not scold or berate but encourage and persuade.

The Homily Is a Liturgical Act

The homily is an integral part of the liturgy. It is not a separate action but an integral part of the Liturgy of the Word intended to prepare the congregation for the Liturgy of the Eucharist. This being so, the preacher should view the homily as part of the community's worship. At the end of the homily the congregation should have a deeper understanding of the Word that has been proclaimed and a renewed thirst for the Eucharist it is about to receive. The congregation should be ready to praise God with renewed fervor and devotion.

The Homily Should Be Clear and Concise

Homilists have five to ten minutes to make their point. If they preach longer, in most instances they will reap diminishing returns. My own practice has been to preach for five to seven minutes (about five or six hundred words). If the point cannot be made in that period of time, it cannot be made. But if the point is to be made, the homily must be clear, concise, persuasive, and passionate. For the homily to be clear and concise, preachers need to think out what they will say. Having written my homilies for forty years, I would argue that the homily needs to be written out, even if the preacher does not take the text to the pulpit.

Preachers who do not write out their homilies should perform this exercise at least once. First, they should ask someone to record and transcribe their homily to a written text. Second, they should analyze the transcribed text and ask if it is clear and concise. If their homily is repetitive and verbose, they have not made their point in a clear and concise manner because they have said too much!

The Homily Needs a Clearly Defined Structure

Like a good sentence, the homily needs structure. Structure reinforces rhetoric and leads to a clear and concise presentation. Every homily ought to have three parts: (1) an introduction, (2) the body of the homily, (3) a conclusion. The body of most homilies will have two parts: (a) an exposition of Scripture and (b) an application of the text to the life of the congregation.

The Introduction Should Be Brief

The introduction should be brief and rarely self-referential. Extended introductions make the body of the homily subservient to the introduction, and they rarely serve the body of the homily. Preachers who make use of self-referential introductions run the risk of preaching about themselves rather than the gospel they are proclaiming. Two or three sentences are sufficient for an effective introduction. Anything beyond that tends to turn the introduction into the homily.

The Exposition of Scripture Should Provide the Background Necessary to Understand the Text

The first part of the body of the homily is an exposition of Scripture. Although this exposition presupposes sound exegesis, it should not be turned into an exegetical lesson. An exposition of Scripture should give the congregation the background necessary to understand the text. In the case of the Pauline homily, this means explaining what occasioned this text and why Paul responded as he did. Thus, it is important for preachers to know why Paul wrote his letters, even if they do not use all of this information in their homily.

The Application Should Explain the Significance of the Text for the Life of the Community

The second part of the body, the application of the homily to the needs of the congregation, is the key element. It is here that the homily stands or falls. The preacher must make the historical and cultural transition from then to now, from the time of Paul to the time of the congregation. The most important question is: How does Paul's proclamation of the gospel apply to the congregation? For example, what is the power of sin in the world today? What is the relation between doing the works of the law in order to justify oneself and our contemporary ethos of achievement and success? How can believers live in the world and yet be a sanctified community? How is the power of the Spirit experienced today? What does it mean to say that Christ will come again? How do believers embody the paradigm of Christ's death and resurrection in their lives?

The Conclusion Should Point to the Eucharist

The conclusion should be brief and formulaic so that the congregation and the preacher know that the homily is coming to a close. Nothing is more revealing of a lack of preparation than the homily that has several endings. Such homilies disclose that the homilist has not thought out the homily. A good conclusion brings the congregation back to the liturgy and prepares them for the Eucharist they are about to receive. As you will see, the conclusions to my homilies are nearly always the same, and they always bring the congregation back to the Eucharist. This means that the congregation that listens to me over a period of time knows when I am ending my homily.

Homilies Are a Record of Our Preaching

Homilies are a record of our growth and development in preaching the gospel. By reminding us of how we preached in the past, they provide us with new ways to preach in the future. There is a value, then, in keeping old homilies. Moreover, one can usually rewrite old homilies for the better. Thus, while it would be irresponsible to preach an old homily without revision, it makes eminent sense to rewrite and revise past material for a new situation.

Homilists Need Criticism and Feedback

Homilies need to be shared and critiqued. While most of us think we are good preachers, few of us have ever had a professional evaluation of our preaching. Homilists will never know how their homilies are received if they do not receive some kind of feedback. One way to get such feedback is to ask parishioners to form a group that will evaluate the homily. By listening to what others have to say, homilists will receive a more objective evaluation of their preaching than they are accustomed to hearing.

Romans in Outline

Since Romans is a complicated letter, it is important to have a sense of the whole before preaching from any part of the letter. What is the gospel that Paul proclaims in this letter? How does the letter cohere and develop? What is the structure of the letter? While the introductions to most commentaries provide answers to these questions, there is no substitute for personal engagement with the text, which comes from reading the text over and over again. Only when preachers read the text repeatedly will they become intimate with it. Only when they become intimate with the text will the text reveal its secrets to them. Accordingly, although there is no substitute for reading the text, I provide a brief outline of Romans followed by a synopsis of its argument and some of the themes that the text offers for preaching.[1]

1. This outline and the synopsis of Romans that follows are taken with permission from my commentary, *Romans*, Paideia (Grand Rapids: Baker Academic, 2010).

The Letter Opening (1:1-17)

Formal greeting and introduction (1:1-7)
Thanksgiving and plans to visit Rome (1:8-15)
The gospel and the revelation of God's righteousness (1:16-17)

I. Gentiles and Jews in the Light of God's Wrath (1:18–3:20)

A. Gentile failure to acknowledge God (1:18-32)
  The revelation of God's wrath (1:18)
  Why God's wrath is being revealed (1:19-23)
    Because humanity is without excuse (1:19-20)
    Because humanity did not honor God as God (1:21-23)
  How God's wrath is being revealed (1:24-31)
    God handed them over to impurity (1:24-25)
    God handed them over to degrading passion (1:26-27)
    God handed them over to their undiscerning mind
      (1:28-31)
  Final condemnation (1:32)

B. God's impartial judgment of Gentiles and Jews (2:1-16)
  God's just and impartial judgment (2:1-11)
  An example of God's impartiality (2:12-16)

C. Jewish failure to observe the law (2:17-29)
  Reliance on the law is insufficient (2:17-24)
  Reliance on circumcision is insufficient (2:25-29)

D. Gentiles and Jews under the power of sin (3:1-20)
  Questions and responses (3:1-8)
  All under the power of sin (3:9-20)

II. Gentiles and Jews in the Light of God's Righteousness (3:21–4:25)

A. The manifestation of God's righteousness apart from the law
  (3:21-26)

B. Boasting excluded (3:27-31)

C. Abraham, the father of all who believe (4:1-25)
  Why Abraham's faith was credited to him as righteousness
    (4:1-8)
  When Abraham's faith was credited to him as righteousness
    (4:9-12)
  Why the promise is based on faith (4:13-17)
  What kind of faith Abraham exhibited (4:18-22)
  Conclusion (4:23-25)

III. The Experience of Salvation in the Light of God's Righteousness (5:1–8:39)

A. Transferred from the realm of sin to the realm of grace (5:1-21)
  Humanity's new relationship to God as its ground for hope (5:1-11)
  The reason for this new relationship and hope (5:12-21)

B. No longer slaves of sin and death (6:1-23)
  Why believers should not remain in sin (6:1-14)
  A change of allegiance from sin to righteousness (6:15-23)

C. Released from a law frustrated by sin (7:1-25)
  An example from the law (7:1-6)
  The law is not sinful (7:7-12)
  The law did not bring death (7:13-23)
  Conclusion (7:24-25)

D. Life and hope in the realm of the Spirit (8:1-39)
  The Spirit as the source of life (8:1-17)
  The Spirit as the source of hope (8:18-30)
  The irrevocable character of God's love (8:31-39)

IV. God's Righteousness and the Destiny of Israel (9:1–11:36)

A. The mystery of divine election (9:1-29)
  Paul's concern for Israel (9:1-5)
  The principle of election (9:6-13)
  A first objection and Paul's response (9:14-18)
  A second objection and Paul's response (9:19-29)

B. The reason for Israel's failure (9:30–10:21)
  Israel's failure to attain righteousness (9:30–10:4)
  The righteousness that comes from faith (10:5-13)
  Israel's disobedience (10:14-21)

C. God's irrevocable call (11:1-36)
  A remnant remains (11:1-6)
  The hardening of "the rest" of Israel (11:7-10)
  The purpose of Israel's misstep (11:11-12)
  A warning to Gentiles (11:13-24)
  The revelation of the mystery of Israel (11:25-32)
  God's inscrutable wisdom (11:33-36)

V. God's Righteousness and the Moral Life of the Justified (12:1–15:13)

A. Love and obedience in the new age (12:1–13:14)
  Paul's fundamental moral exhortation (12:1-2)

Living as one body in Christ (12:3-8)
Genuine love (12:9-21)
Subordination to those in authority (13:1-7)
Love as the fulfillment of the law (13:8-10)
The moral life in light of the end (13:11-14)

B. Receiving each other according to the example of Christ
(14:1–15:13)

An exhortation not to judge each other (14:1-12)
An exhortation not to scandalize each other (14:13-23)
An exhortation to support the weak (15:1-6)
An exhortation to receive each other (15:7-13)

The Letter Closing (15:14–16:27)

Paul's travel plans (15:14-33)
Commendation of Phoebe and greetings to those in Rome (16:1-16)
A warning (16:17-20)
Greetings from those with Paul (16:21-23)
Grace (16:24)
Doxology (16:25-27)

A Synopsis of Romans

The Letter Opening (1:1-17)

Romans begins with a letter opening in which Paul introduces himself, summarizes the gospel he preaches, announces his desire to visit the Romans, and explains why he is not ashamed of the gospel. In explaining why he is not ashamed of the gospel, Paul announces the theme that underlies his gospel: the righteousness of God, by which he means God's saving justice as revealed in Christ for the salvation of all, Gentile as well as Jew. This carefully constructed letter opening is longer than any other Pauline greeting because Paul is introducing himself to a community he did not establish, most of whose members have never seen or heard him, although some have heard rumors and scandalous remarks about his law-free gospel. In the letter closing Paul will return to several of the themes he announces in the letter opening, especially his apostolic commission and plans to visit Rome, thereby enclosing the "body" of the letter in a "frame" that consists of an opening and closing that interpret each other as well as the entire letter.

Gentiles and Jews in the Light of God's Wrath (1:18–3:20)

Having announced that he is not ashamed of the gospel because it reveals God's righteousness, Paul proclaims that the wrath of God is presently being revealed against the impiety and unrighteousness of those who are suppressing the truth of God. The righteousness and the wrath of God can be compared to two sides of a coin. "The wrath of God is to unbelief the discovery of His righteousness, for God is not mocked. The wrath of God is the righteousness of God—apart from and without Christ" (Karl Barth, *The Epistle to the Romans*, 1933, 43).

Paul's purpose in this part of Romans is to show that all, without exception, Jew as well as Gentile, are in need of the saving righteousness that God has manifested in Christ because all, Jew as well as Gentile, are under the domination of a cosmic power that Paul identifies as "sin." Although Paul will not explain until chapter 5 how "sin" attained this status, this part of Romans seeks to persuade Paul's audience of the sinful plight in which humanity finds itself and so its need for the saving righteousness that God reveals in Christ.

Paul develops his argument in four movements. First, he points to the failure of the Gentile world to acknowledge the truth and glory of God, even though it knew something of God from the created world (1:18-32). Consequently, God is presently manifesting his wrath against the sinful Gentile world by handing the Gentiles over to their own sinfulness so that the punishment of sin is to live in sin. Second, before turning to the situation of the Jewish world, Paul points to the impartiality of God (2:1-16). God does not judge people on the basis of who they are but on the basis of what they do or fail to do. Having reminded his audience of God's impartiality, in the third movement Paul indicts the Jewish world for its failure to do the law in which it rightly boasts, for reliance on the law and circumcision are insufficient if one does not do the law (2:17-29). Paul begins the fourth movement by asking, if this is the situation in which the Jewish world finds itself, then what advantage is there in being a Jew (3:1-20)? After assuring his audience that there are many advantages, he comes to the climax of his argument. Although the Jewish world enjoys the advantage of the law and circumcision, it is no better off because all are under the power of "sin" (3:9). Consequently no one will be justified before God by doing the works of the law (3:20) because all are under the power of "sin."

Although this description of the human plight may seem excessive, Paul is *not* giving a sociological analysis of the human condition. Standing on a higher mountain, he is *revealing* the situation of humanity apart from Christ when the human situation is analyzed in light of the saving righteousness that the gospel proclaims.

Gentiles and Jews in the Light of God's Righteousness (3:21–4:25)

Having argued that all, Jews as well as Gentiles, find themselves in a predicament from which they cannot free themselves because they are under the power of "sin," Paul returns to the theme of God's saving righteousness, which he introduced in 1:17. In one of the most important passages of Romans, he declares that God has manifested his saving righteousness in Christ's death on the cross. This death resulted in redemption, justification, atonement, and the forgiveness of sins (3:21-26). Consequently, there is no room for boasting before God because all, Jew as well as Gentile, are justified on the basis of faith apart from doing the works of the Mosaic law (3:27-31). To show that his gospel confirms the law rather than nullifies it, in chapter 4 Paul recounts the story of Abraham. In light of the gospel he exegetes the text of Gen 15:6: "Abraham believed God, and it was credited to him as righteousness" (Rom 4:3). Noting that God acquitted Abraham on the basis of Abraham's trusting faith in God's promises before Abraham was circumcised, Paul presents Abraham as a model for Gentiles as well as Jews who walk in the way of faith that Abraham exhibited when he was still uncircumcised. Paul concludes this chapter with a description of Abraham's faith that was a type of resurrection faith inasmuch as Abraham believed God's promise even when his body and the womb of his wife Sarah were, for all practical purposes, dead. Such faith shows that Abraham already believed in the God and Father of Jesus Christ who raises the dead.

The Experience of Salvation in the Light of God's Righteousness (5:1–8:39)

After establishing the universal need for salvation and show-ing that God has responded to this need by manifesting his saving righteousness in Jesus Christ, Paul provides his audience with an extended discussion of the meaning and implication of God's righteousness for the Christian life. Paul develops this part of Romans in four movements. In the first he describes how the justi-fied have been transferred from the realm of "sin" to the realm of God's "grace" (5:1-21). This movement begins with a description of the new situation in which believers find themselves (5:1-11): they are at peace with God because they have been justified and reconciled to God. Having been justified and reconciled to God, they can be all the more confident that they will be saved. Accord-ingly, believers live in hope of final salvation, a theme to which Paul will return at the end of chapter 8. To explain how this situa-tion came about and how sin entered the world, Paul draws a comparison between Adam's act of disobedience that brought "sin" and "death" into the world, and Christ's singular act of obedience that brought "grace" and "life" into the world.

The second movement of Paul's discussion deals with the problem of sin in the Christian life (6:1-23). Paul's gospel proclaims that when sin increased, God's grace increased all the more (5:20); doesn't this imply that there is no need to stop sinning? Paul re-sponds to this objection in two ways. First, he argues that believers died to sin when they participated in Christ's death through their baptism. Consequently, they have died to the power of sin over their lives (6:1-14). Second, he reminds them that they are no longer slaves of "sin," which pays a wage of "death," but slaves of righteous-ness that gives them the gift of eternal life (6:15-23). Consequently, although it is possible for the justified to sin, continuing to sin is incongruous with the gospel that Paul preaches.

In the third movement of this part of the letter Paul takes up the question of the Mosaic Law (7:1-25). Does Paul's gospel imply that there is something sinful about the law (7:7)? Did the law bring people to death (7:13)? Paul emphatically denies these charges against his gospel by affirming that the law is holy (7:12) and spiritual (7:14). The culprit is not the law but the power of indwelling sin that frustrates the human person's desire to do what is good. In one of the most important and disputed passages of Romans, Paul describes the plight of the conflicted self that knows God's will but cannot do it because of the power of indwelling sin (7:13-23). The chapter comes to its climax with a cry of desperation: "Miserable one that I am! Who will deliver me from this mortal body?" (7:24).

In chapter 8, the fourth movement of Paul's argument, the Apostle answers this cry. What the law could not do, God has done by sending his own Son into the realm of the flesh to combat "sin" in its own realm. After explaining how God dealt with sin by sending his own Son (8:1-4), Paul describes the new life of those who are in the realm of God's Spirit rather than in the realm of the flesh (8:5-17). Empowered by the Spirit, they can now live in a way that is pleasing to God. In the second half of chapter 8 (8:18-30), Paul returns to the theme of eschatological hope that he introduced in 5:1-11. Because the justified have received the gift of God's Spirit, they can be confident that God, who raised Jesus from the dead, will raise them as well. In addition to this, Paul affirms that the whole of creation is waiting for the revelation of God's children (which will occur at the general resurrection of the dead) so that creation itself can be set free from its bondage to futility. The chapter ends with a dramatic statement of God's irrevocable love for the justified that assures them that nothing can separate them from God's love for them (8:31-39).

God's Righteousness and the Destiny of Israel (9:1–11:36)

After the ecstatic statement of confidence that concludes chapter 8, it might appear that Paul has said all that needs to be said about the righteousness of God. But this is not the case. Before he can complete his proclamation of God's saving righteousness, Paul must deal with two issues: (1) the failure of Israel to believe in the saving righteousness that God has revealed in Christ, and (2) the moral life of the justified. Paul deals with the first of these issues in Romans 9–11, and with the second in 12:1–15:13.

As nearly all contemporary commentators insist, Romans 9–11 is an integral part of Paul's exposition of the gospel since the fundamental question that drives the discussion is the faithfulness and integrity of God: has God been faithful to Israel? Given the content of Paul's gospel, which proclaims justification on the basis of faith rather than on the basis of doing the works of the Mosaic Law, it might appear that: (1) God's ways have changed, (2) God has not been faithful to the covenant promises made to Israel, and (3) God has rejected his people. If this is the case, God is no longer reliable; God can no longer be trusted; God is not righteous. Accordingly, Romans 9–11 is Paul's most profound discussion about God.

Paul develops this part of Romans in three movements. In the first, he considers the mystery of divine election by which God created Israel and continues to work on Israel's behalf (9:1-29). After expressing his deep concern for his people, Paul reviews the history of Israel to show how God created and sustained Israel on the basis of divine election (9:6-13). He then confronts two objections to the principle of election: first, election implies injustice on God's part (9:14-18); second, God should not find fault because no one can oppose God's will (9:19-29). In response to the first objection he recalls the account of the hardening of Pharaoh to show that everything depends on God's mercy. In response to the second he argues that it is not the place of the creature to question the Creator. He then explains that just as God created Israel on the basis of election, so God is presently creating a people from the Gentiles as well the Jews. The word of God has not failed (9:6), for God is acting as God has always acted, on the basis of election and mercy.

In the second movement of his argument Paul insists that the problem is not with God but with Israel's refusal to recognize God's saving righteousness revealed in Christ (9:30–10:21). The movement begins by highlighting the paradox that the Gentiles, who did not pursue righteousness, attained it, whereas Israel, which zealously pursued righteousness on the basis of the law, failed to attain that righteousness (9:30-33). Paul's response is that Israel's zeal for the law was misguided because it did not recognize that Christ was the goal and terminus of the law. Consequently, Israel found itself pursuing its own righteousness rather than the righteousness God revealed in Christ (10:1-4). Paul concludes this movement by describing what he means by the righteousness that comes from faith (10:5-13) and by affirming that Israel has indeed heard the gospel (10:14-21). As Isaiah prophesied long ago, Israel has been, and remains, disobedient. The problem, then, is not the unfaithfulness of God but the disobedience of Israel.

In the third movement Paul affirms God's irrevocable call of Israel (11:1-36). God has not rejected Israel, for even though Israel has been disobedient, a faithful remnant remains, but a hardening has come upon the rest of Israel (11:1-10). However, this hardening is part of the divine plan. By it salvation has come to the Gentiles in order to make disobedient Israel jealous so that it will embrace the righteousness revealed in Jesus Christ (11:11-12). Consequently, Paul warns his Gentile readers who have been grafted into the olive tree, which is Israel, not to boast against unbelieving Israel because God is able to graft those who have not believed into the tree from which they were cut off (11:13-24). After this warning Paul reveals a mystery: all Israel will be saved (11:25-32). Filled with awe as he contemplates the divine plan that will bring Jew and Gentile to salvation, Paul concludes this part of his letter with a hymn-like passage that celebrates God's inscrutable wisdom (11:33-36).

God's Righteousness and the Moral Life of the Justified (12:1–15:13)

Although Paul has completed what is sometimes called the "doctrinal" portion of his letter, he has not finished his exposition of the gospel. In the final part of Romans he must still draw out the implications of his gospel for everyday life. Paul develops this part in two movements. First, he presents the Romans with a general moral exhortation (12:1–13:14) before addressing a concrete issue pertinent to the Roman house congregations (14:1–15:13).

Paul sounds the leitmotif for his moral exhortation in 12:1-2 when he presents the moral life as an act of worship. The moral life that Paul envisions is integrally connected to the gospel he preaches inasmuch as it is a grateful response to what God has done in Christ. Consequently, living a morally good life becomes a way in which the justified offer themselves as living sacrifices to God. Following this initial exhortation Paul embarks upon the first part of his paraenesis (12:3–13:14). Here he encourages the

Romans to work for the good of each other by exercising the gifts that have been entrusted to them for their mutual benefit. He then provides the Romans with a description of genuine love, exhorting them not to avenge themselves but to leave retribution to God. Next, Paul exhorts the Romans to be subject to those in authority and pay taxes to those to whom they are due. He concludes this section by reminding his audience that all of the commandments find their fulfillment in the commandment to love one's neighbor, and he encourages them to prepare themselves for the struggle that the moral life entails since the day of their salvation is at hand.

In the second section of his paraenesis Paul addresses the problem of the "weak" and the "strong" (14:1–15:13). Although commentators differ in the way they interpret the historical situation behind this section, the general thrust of Paul's argument suggests that he is addressing opposing factions among the Roman Christians, some of whom continue to practice certain dietary and calendar prescriptions of the law, and others who do not. Although Paul identifies himself as belonging to the strong, he exhorts the strong not to scandalize the weak and, if necessary, to curb their freedom in these matters. The entire section comes to a climax when Paul calls upon the weak and the strong to welcome each other as Christ welcomed them (15:7-13).

The Letter Closing (15:14–16:27)

The letter closing returns to several of the themes that Paul introduced in the letter opening. In doing so it forms a "frame" around the body of the letter. It begins with Paul repeating his plans to visit Rome, which he announced in the letter opening (15:14-33). But this time he reveals that his visit is only one stage of a greater journey that will bring him to Spain, where he will open a new mission. Before he comes to Rome and goes to Spain, however, he must travel to Jerusalem to deliver the collection he has been taking up among his Gentile congregations for the poor among the Jewish believers in Jerusalem. After announcing his travel plans Paul commends Phoebe (who may be the bearer of the letter) to the Romans before greeting several of the Roman Christians (16:1-16). The letter concludes with a warning about those who would cause divisions (16:17-20), greetings from those who are with Paul at Corinth (16:21-23), a grace-wish that is not present in all manuscripts (16:24), and a benediction that is found in different places in the manuscript tradition (16:25-27).

Themes for Preaching from Romans[2]

The Righteousness of God

Romans is first and foremost about God. To be sure, humanity plays an important role in this letter, but God is the principal actor in the drama of salvation that Paul describes. The centrality of God in Romans is evident from the outset when Paul announces the letter's theme: the righteousness of God.

> For I am not ashamed of the gospel. It is the power of God for the salvation of everyone who believes: for Jew first, and then Greek. For in it is revealed *the righteousness of God* from faith to faith; as it is written, "The one who is righteous by faith will live." (1:16-17)

By the "the righteousness of God" Paul means *God's own righteousness,* God's uprightness, God's fidelity, God's covenant loyalty or, as the Revised English Bible puts it, "God's way of righting wrong."

Paul repeats the theme of God's righteousness in Rom 3:21-26. In this text he explains that since all have sinned, God manifested his saving righteousness in Jesus Christ. This means that through Christ, God definitively dealt with sin, thereby manifesting his uprightness and covenant loyalty. Although God manifested his righteousness apart from the law so that it would be available to all people on the basis of faith, Paul insists that the law and the prophets testify to God's saving righteousness, thereby showing God's faithfulness in dealing with his covenant people.

The starting point for preaching from Romans is an understanding of the utter reliability of God who fulfills his promises through Jesus Christ. Since Romans is about God, those who

---

2. This section is a revised version of material originally published in *Church* 18 (2002): 50–53.

preach from Romans will inevitably find themselves preaching about God, whom Paul describes as the God who justifies the ungodly, the God who raises the dead, the God of hope, the God of peace, the God who reveals himself as faithful and new in Jesus Christ. To preach from Romans, then, is to preach about God.

The Human Condition and the Power of Sin

In addition to being a letter about God, Romans is a letter about the human condition. Looking at humanity from the perspective of God's saving righteousness, Paul argues that humanity finds itself in a sinful predicament from which it cannot extricate itself. Consequently, after announcing that the theme of his letter is the righteousness of God, Paul turns to the human condition apart from God's saving righteousness and announces that "the wrath of God is indeed being revealed from heaven against every impiety and wickedness of those who suppress the truth by their wickedness" (1:18).

The "wrath of God" is not to be mistaken for an emotion of God, as if God becomes angry. The wrath of God *is* the righteousness of God in the face of sin. Paul describes this wrath in terms of God handing humanity over to its own devices so that sinful humanity wallows in its own sinfulness. Thus the punishment for sin is sin. Having worshiped the creature rather than the creator, humanity finds itself alienated from God.

In Rom 1:18–3:20 Paul describes this predicament in which the whole of humanity finds itself when it is alienated from God. Toward the end of this section Paul proclaims "all are under the domination of sin" (3:9). Consequently, "no human being will be justified in his [God's] sight by observing the law" (3:20).

According to Paul sin is a cosmic power and force that controls our lives. It is a power from which only God's grace can free us. One of the most important services that preachers can do is to make their congregations aware of the human condition apart from Christ. To do so they must be able to reveal and expose how the cosmic power of sin is still at work in the world today, for example, market capitalism that has no regard for the poor and needy, consumerism that sees salvation in the here and how, racism that denies the impartiality of God, and addictions of all kinds.

Justified by God's Grace

If we cannot be "justified" before God on the basis of what we do, then we must rely on God to justify and acquit us on the basis of his grace and favor manifested in Jesus Christ. Justification by faith means that God graciously "acquits" us, pronouncing us "innocent" because of what God has done for us in Jesus Christ rather than what we have done for God.

Justification, then, is a gracious pronouncement of acquittal that only God can make. No one can "earn" such an acquittal; no one is worthy of it. But when God pronounces such an acquittal, God rectifies and justifies sinful humanity so that it stands in the correct and proper relationship to God, who is the faithful and reliable covenant God of Israel, the God and Father of Jesus Christ.

This teaching about justification by faith is not familiar to most Roman Catholics. But what it proclaims is at the core of what Catholics believe about God's grace. We are not put in a right relationship with God by what we do but by what God has done for us in Christ. We are not reconciled with God because of any good deeds we have done but because of the gracious love God extends to us in Christ. We are justified and reconciled on the basis of God's grace, and because we are already justified and reconciled we can hope, with assurance, that we will be saved.

Those who preach from Romans should find a way to remind their congregations again and again that all is grace, sheer unmerited grace.

Faith in God Who Raises the Dead

If we are justified by God's grace, how should we respond to God? The answer Paul gives in Romans is trusting faith in God who raises the dead. This is why Paul writes, "For we consider that a person is justified by faith apart from works of the law" (3:28).

To say that a person is justified by faith apart from works of the law means that our salvation is not determined by success or achievement, accomplishment or status, pedigree or background. Thus Paul strikes a mortal blow to the ethos of many contemporary Americans—Christians included. Rather than achievement, the response God seeks is the kind of faith Abraham manifested when the great patriarch believed in God's promises that he (Abraham) would be the father of a multitude of people.

Paul describes the nature of Abraham's faith in Romans 4. This faith cannot be reduced to believing in a creed, nor is it sufficient to call it faith in God. Rather, it is faith in *the God who raises the dead*. Such faith trusts that God who is faithful can and will do what humanity cannot. Such faith trusts in the utter reliability and dependability of God. Such faith hopes even when there is no human reason to hope (see Rom 4:18).

Those who preach from Romans will have an opportunity to discuss the nature of this faith. In doing so they will teach their congregations that faith is an act of total obedience to God. Such faith trusts and relies on the God who raises the dead.

A New Adam, a New Humanity

Those who entrust themselves to what God has done in Christ are justified and reconciled to God. Because they are justified and reconciled to God, they belong to a new humanity, whose head is Jesus Christ, the obedient Son of God, the new Adam (Romans 5). Whereas the old Adam rebelled against God, thereby introducing a history of sin and death into the world, the new Adam obediently carried out God's will, thereby inaugurating a history of sin and grace. Ever since Christ, then, life has been a choice between solidarity with the old Adam or solidarity with the new Adam. There is no middle ground, and to this very day every human being must choose to be in solidarity with one or the other.

In preaching Romans preachers have an opportunity to remind people that they are no longer in the old Adam, the realm of sin and death, but in the new Adam, the realm of grace and life. The church is the place where the new Adam should be manifest to a world that is still in the old Adam.

The Power of God's Spirit

Paul argues that previous to the coming of Christ, humanity could not do what God's law required. Those under the law knew what the law required, and they even wanted to do what the law required. But because of the power of sin, they dwelt in the old Adam, the realm of sin and death. Consequently, they could not do what the law required. Paul describes this situation in Romans 7, arguing that although the Mosaic Law was holy, good, and spiritual, it was frustrated by the power of "sin" (Romans 6–7). Even those who knew the will of God did not obey the law.

But in chapter 8 Paul describes how God has remedied this situation by sending his only Son—the new Adam—in the form of sinful flesh to condemn "sin" in the flesh. Consequently, we find ourselves in the sphere of God's Spirit. We live by the Spirit; we walk by the Spirit. It is the Spirit that fulfills in us the just requirement of the law. More than that, this Spirit is the firstfruits of a final redemption that is yet to come.

Romans 8 plays a central role in Paul's argument by indicating how Christians live their new life. They no longer live in the realm of "the flesh," which is Paul's metaphor for what is merely mortal and destined for destruction. They live in the realm of the Spirit, God's own Spirit, which makes them alive and gives them the power to do what they cannot do of themselves.

Romans 8 provides preachers with an opportunity to speak about life in the Spirit and remind the congregation that they now live in the realm of God's grace that enables them to do what they could not do before.

The Moral Life of the Justified

Because believers dwell in the realm of the Spirit they can and must live a morally good life. Justification by faith apart from the works of the law, then, is not a license for people "to believe" and then do whatever they want. It is not an excuse for an immoral life. On the contrary, the justified live a morally good life precisely because they live in the realm of God's Spirit.

Paul devotes 12:1–15:13 to a description of the moral life of believers. Believers present themselves as "a living sacrifice, holy and pleasing to God" (12:1). The moral life of obedience becomes their way of worshiping God. Empowered by the Spirit, believers fulfill the law through the love commandment, which encompasses the whole of the law (13:8-10).

In addition to chapters 12:1–15:13, in which Paul provides specific moral instruction, preachers will want to study what Paul writes about the moral life in chapter 6. In chapter 6 he takes up a challenge to his gospel: since grace abounded all the more where sin abounded, perhaps the justified should continue to sin all the more! In response to this challenge, Paul argues that believers have died to sin by their baptism, which was a baptism into Christ's death. Consequently, sin should no longer rule over their lives. To be sure, believers can still sin, but they are no longer obliged to sin. Having entered into Christ's death through their baptism, they have died to the power of sin over their lives.

The Nature of Salvation

Paul is firmly convinced that believers are *already* justified and reconciled to God because of what God has done in Christ. But he is also aware that they are *not yet* saved.

For Paul, salvation is a cosmic event that will only be accomplished at the general resurrection of the dead when Christ's brothers and sisters are raised from the dead to enjoy the glory that he, the risen Lord, already enjoys. The salvation of the justified and reconciled will bring about the renewal of creation. This is why Paul writes that all creation is waiting with eager longing for the revelation of the children of God that will occur at the general resurrection of the dead. Thus believers are saved in hope—in hope for their resurrection from the dead.

Romans provides preachers with an opportunity to discuss the cosmic scope of God's plan of salvation that includes the whole of the created world.

The Future of Israel

What is the role of Israel in God's plan of salvation? Does Paul's gospel, which proclaims the "the righteousness of God," have any place for the covenant people of Israel? Or has the covenant been revoked and Israel rejected? Such a scenario would surely throw into question the faithfulness of God. But Paul will have no part in this. In three of the most moving chapters of the New Testament (Romans 9–11), Paul struggles over the refusal of his people to accept Jesus as the Messiah. But at the end of these chapters Paul's verdict is clear: God has not rejected his people (11: 2) and, in a way known only to God, "all Israel will be saved" (11:26). Thus, Paul's teaching on "the righteousness of God" clearly shows that there is no room for anti-Jewish or anti-Semitic sentiments among those justified by grace.

In a world that is always tempted to be anti-Semitic, Romans provides preachers with an opportunity to speak about the "mystery of Israel" and God's irrevocable election of Israel as his people.

Preaching from Romans on Sunday

During Year A in the cycle of Sunday readings, the Roman Lectionary provides a semi-continuous reading of Romans from the ninth to the twenty-fourth Sundays of Ordinary Time, a period of four months. Although the reading is semi-continuous inasmuch as the Lectionary omits large portions of Romans, the Lectionary does follow the order of the letter. Consequently, in addition to giving attention to the readings of the Lectionary, preachers must be attentive to those portions of the text from which the Lectionary does not read if they hope to understand the larger context of each reading. One way to do this is to take a New Testament and highlight or underline the portion of Romans that the Lectionary uses. This will enable preachers to see the texts that the Lectionary passes over. This exercise has the added advantage of making preachers aware of the wider context of the passage to which they must pay attention in preparing their homily.

In anticipation of the ground that we will cover, I begin by summarizing the texts of Romans in Year A of the Sunday Lectionary.

Ninth Sunday (Rom 3:21-25, 28)

God's saving righteousness. This is Paul's most important statement about God's righteousness. It should be read in light of his statement in 1:16-17, which is the first appearance of this theme in the letter. This text comes after Paul's relentless description of human sin and failure on the part of both Gentiles and Jews (1:18–3:20).

Tenth Sunday (Rom 4:18-25)

God who raises the dead. After Paul has recounted how God has justified humanity through the death of his Son, in Romans 4 he describes the kind of faith the justified need if they are to appropriate what God has done for them. Abraham's faith anticipates the resurrection faith of the Christian inasmuch as Abraham believed *in God who raises the dead.* This text is an opportunity to speak about faith. To preach this text, however, one must read through and reflect on the whole of Romans 4.

Eleventh Sunday (Rom 5:6-11)

God's proven love for us. After describing the nature of faith, Paul celebrates the new situation of the justified, who can be confident of the love that God has for them. In this passage, Paul describes God's love for us. Christ died for us when we were still sinners. Christ's love for us is a proof of God's love for us. Note that Paul says that we are *already* justified, *already* reconciled, but we are *not yet saved.* This will only occur at the resurrection of the dead. Present justification and reconciliation, however, are an assurance of future salvation.

Twelfth Sunday (Rom 5:12-15)

The origin of sin. In the second half of chapter 5 Paul explains the reason for the hope that he has described in the first part of the chapter. Christ's obedience has countered Adam's disobedience. Paul begins a comparison that he does not complete (5:1). To make sense of this comparison, see the conclusion of the comparison in 5:18-19. Paul is talking about two progenitors of humanity: Adam and Christ. We stand in solidarity with either one or the other.

Thirteenth Sunday (Rom 6:3-4, 8-11)

Baptized into Christ's death. The challenge of this text is to remind believers that they have died to sin because they have been baptized into Christ's death. Baptism is not a mere washing and cleansing of sin, it is a participation in the historical event of Christ's death. When this happens, sin no longer rules over the believer. The task of the preacher is to remind believers that in their baptism they entered into Christ's own death, thereby dying to an old way of life.

Fourteenth Sunday (Rom 8:9, 11-13)

The spirit and the flesh. This Sunday begins a series of five readings on the role of the Spirit in the life of the believer. When Paul says that we are not in the flesh, he means that we no longer belong to the realm of sinful humanity that Adam inaugurated by his trespass. Rather, we belong to the realm of redeemed humanity that Christ, the new Adam, inaugurated. We belong to the realm or sphere of the Spirit. The flesh is all that is mortal and weak. The Spirit is all that is immortal and strong.

Fifteenth Sunday (Rom 8:18-23)

The fullness of salvation. This text highlights the cosmic dimension of the salvation that awaits believers. All creation is waiting for the moment when the redeemed will be revealed as God's children. This will happen at the general resurrection of the dead when creation will be redeemed as well. In Paul's view, redemption is cosmic in scope.

Sixteenth Sunday (Rom 8:26-27)

Discerning the mystery. Here Paul speaks of the Spirit as the one who comes to the aid of believers, since they do not know how to pray as they ought. The Spirit intercedes for them, thereby making their prayers effective before God. The Spirit empowers us to pray as we ought.

Seventeenth Sunday (Rom 8:28-30)

All will be well. Paul establishes an interesting "ladder of ascent." First, he says that God foreknew us, predestined us, and conformed us to the image of his Son. Then he says God predestined, called, justified, and glorified us. Paul affirms that we have been part of God's plan of salvation from all eternity. Nothing has happened by chance. Everything that has happened is part of God's plan for our salvation.

Eighteenth Sunday (Rom 8:35, 37-39)

Forever united with Christ. This is Paul's conclusion to chapter 8. Here he affirms his absolute conviction that nothing can separate those who believe in Christ from God. This conviction is based on his confidence in the faithfulness of God, which God has manifested in Christ. A text such as this should be preached in light of all that Paul has said in Romans 8.

Nineteenth Sunday (Rom 9:1-5)

Paul's love for his people. This is the beginning of Paul's discussion about Israel and the faithfulness of God. One needs to read the whole of Romans 9–11 to understand what Paul is saying here. He is filled with anguish that his people have not accepted the Messiah, but he is confident that Israel will be saved. A homily on Romans 9–11 is an opportunity to speak of the continuing love God has for the people of Israel. It is an occasion to show that there is no room for anti-Semitism in the Christian life.

Twentieth Sunday (Rom 11:13-15, 29-32)

God's irrevocable call. This is a warning to Gentile Christians (to us!) not to become proud because of Israel's failure. It is important to read the entire parable (11:13-24). Paul insists that God's gifts and call are irrevocable. Israel remains the chosen people of God.

Twenty-First Sunday (Rom 11:33-36)

God's mysterious ways. This concluding doxology needs to be read in light of the entire context of Romans 9–11. Paul expresses his amazement at the mystery of Israel. God will always be faithful to his people, even though Paul cannot fully understand what is presently occurring.

Twenty-Second Sunday (Rom 12:1-2)

The moral life as an act of worship. This is the beginning of Paul's moral exhortation, which continues through chapter 15. Paul presents the moral life as an act of worship. Those who have been renewed can now live the moral life because they have been transformed by the Spirit. Believers act in a particular way because of God's redemptive work in them. The moral life, then, is an act of worship made possible by God's redemptive work in Christ.

Twenty-Third Sunday (Rom 13:8-10)

Love, the fulfillment of the law. This is Paul's summary of how the Christian fulfills the law through the love commandment. Christians are no longer required to do all the prescriptions of the Mosaic Law. They *fulfill* the law by the love commandment. Those who practice love *fulfill* what the law requires.

Twenty-Fourth Sunday (Rom 14:7-9)

The Lord of the living and of the dead. This is part of a discussion about the weak and the strong that begins at 14:1 and continues through 15:13. The point of the discussion is that the strong and the weak are to welcome each other as Christ welcomed them. This text could be used to bring instruction and healing to a divided congregation.

God's Saving Righteousness
Romans 3:21-25, 28

Before the Homily

The Lectionary's first reading from Romans begins with a text that is found toward the end of chapter 3. This means that the congregation has not heard the argument of the first three chapters of this letter, chapters in which Paul describes the situation of the Gentile and Jewish world apart from God's saving righteousness (1:18–3:20). Apart from God's saving righteousness, which is revealed and proclaimed in the gospel, all have sinned—Jew as well as Gentile—because all are under the power of sin (3:9). Accordingly, all—Jew as well as Gentile—are in need of the saving grace of God that was manifested on the cross.

The text for today's reading comes at a climatic moment in Romans. In Rom 1:16-17 Paul affirms that he is not ashamed of the gospel because the gospel reveals God's saving righteousness for all who believe in it. Then in Rom 1:18–3:20 he describes the situation of Gentiles and Jews apart from God's saving righteousness: all have sinned and so all are liable to God's wrath, by which Paul means God's just judgment of sin. Finally, in the text for today's reading, Paul returns to the theme of God's righteousness that he introduced in Rom 1:16-17. But this time he deals with the theme in a more expansive way.

This is a central text in Paul's argument because it celebrates the theme of this letter: the saving righteousness of God, by which Paul means God's saving grace, God's covenant loyalty, God's way of effecting salvation for sinners. As you can see from my outline of Romans (pp. 8–10), this text occurs at the beginning of the second part of Romans, which I have called "Gentiles and Jews in the Light of God's Righteousness" (3:21–4:25). Although the text from the Lectionary is Rom 3:21-25, 28, preachers will do well to take into consideration the whole unit, which consists of Rom 3:21-31.

On first reading this is a rather intimidating text that is highly abstract, dealing with the concepts of "the righteousness of God," "justification," "redemption," and "expiation." Thus homilists will find themselves struggling with one of the most important issues in Pauline theology: justification by faith apart from doing the works of the Mosaic Law. Despite the abstract nature of these concepts, it is possible to preach this text in a way that is accessible to the congregation. In the homily that follows I have focused on the way that God's saving righteousness in Christ breaks down those human distinctions that separate us from each other. In doing so I am talking about the Pauline doctrine of justification without employing the language of justification. This is not the only possibility for preaching the text, but it is the way that I began my preaching of Romans.

The Homily

Introduction. Everyday we draw distinctions between ourselves and other people. For example, I say *I am* of Italian-Lithuanian extraction; *I am* a Roman Catholic priest; *I am* a university professor. In making these distinctions, I separate myself from certain groups, and I identify myself with others. When I make these distinctions, I also intimate that I am different from others: *perhaps* a little better, *perhaps* a little smarter, *perhaps* a little more important.

Exposition. But in today's second reading, from his great letter to the Romans, the Apostle Paul abolishes these distinctions that we would make. He levels the playing field by declaring "there is no distinction; all have sinned and are deprived of God. They are justified freely by his grace."

Application. Consider what the Apostle is saying. From the point of view of the gospel, there is no distinction between human beings; for, in the light of the gospel, it is apparent that all, without exception, have sinned.

We know this. We experience this every day. But we rarely consider its consequences. *Because we have sinned,* we have alienated ourselves from God. *Because we have sinned,* we are like everyone else. *Because we have sinned,* all the distinctions by which we separate ourselves from each other are meaningless. For in this matter that matters most, there is no distinction—we have all sinned.

Consider again what Paul writes. All have sinned, and all are deprived of God's glory. Therefore, all are justified freely by God's grace through the redemption we have in Jesus Christ. This is technical language, but what it means is vital for our lives. *Because we have sinned,* God has done what we could not do—God has forgiven us. *Because we have sinned,* God has done what we could not do—God has acquitted us, declared us innocent; God has justified us in the court that ultimately matters, the court of God. *Because we have sinned*—God has done what we could not do. God has redeemed us by the blood of his own Son; God has freed us from the power of sin.

This is why Paul says that a person is justified by faith apart from works of the law. Again, this is technical language. It is not the kind of language with which we are familiar. But its meaning is vital for our Christian lives. *There is nothing we have done, there is nothing we can do,* that enables us to earn our salvation. The salvation we enjoy in Christ is a free gift from a generous and gracious God who manifests his love for us in his Son, Jesus Christ.

This means that even though there are differences among us, there is no distinction in God's eyes. In the light of the gospel, we are in the same predicament from which we cannot free ourselves. We are in need of God's grace. And because we are, God freely and graciously bestows that grace upon us through his Son, Jesus Christ.

Conclusion. Setting aside every distinction that separates us from each other, we partake of this Eucharist that breaks down every barrier that separates us from each other, and from God.

After the Homily

The introduction to this homily is self-referential, and in this respect it is not the way in which I normally begin a homily. But in this case, a few self-referential statements seemed in order since I wanted to focus on the text "there is no distinction, all have sinned." Accordingly, I used three examples from my own life (which most parishioners already knew about me) in order to show that when we draw distinctions we separate ourselves from each other. These self-referential statements, by which I distinguish myself from others, are purposely intended to put me in a negative light, as trying to present myself as more important than others.

This particular homily does not contain a great deal of exposition. While I could have introduced the main themes of the letter to the Romans in this initial homily on Romans, I decided to focus on a single theme instead: there is no distinction between us when we stand before God. Accordingly, after explaining how we can draw distinctions that separate us from each other, I explain how God has leveled the playing field. There is no distinction between us before God because, apart from the gospel, all of us are in need of God's saving grace.

Having announced my theme, I begin the process of applying the gospel to the life of the congregation. First, I have tried to remind the congregation of the experience of sinfulness that we have all experienced at one time or another. All of us, without exception, have sinned. Second, having reminded the congregation of this experience of sinfulness, I turn to the experience of forgiveness. In addition to the experience of sinfulness, each of us has also experienced the grace of forgiveness that we have not earned and could not possibly merit. This allows me to introduce the doctrine of justification toward the end of the homily where I explain that there is nothing we have done, nothing that we can do, nothing that enables us to "earn" our salvation. Having made these three points (sinfulness, forgiveness, and justification), I return to my central theme: there is no distinction between us because we have all sinned and been freely justified by God's grace.

This particular homily contains a number of phrases (which I have italicized) that I have repeated for the purpose of rhetorical effect.

The homily ends with a brief conclusion that reminds the congregation of the Eucharist they are about to receive. Here I have related the Eucharist to the Pauline teaching of justification by faith. Just as God's work of justification breaks down those barriers that separate us from each other, so the Eucharist breaks down every barrier that separates us from each other and from God.

God Who Raises the Dead
Romans 4:18-25

Before the Homily

At the end of chapter three, Paul raises an objection to his teaching on justification that we heard in last week's reading. In that reading he affirmed that a person is justified (put in a right relation with God) on the basis of faith rather than on the basis of doing the works of the Mosaic Law. But if this is the case, doesn't this imply that Paul is doing away with the Mosaic Law? In response to this objection to his gospel, Paul affirms that his teaching on justification by faith establishes and supports the true meaning of the law.

To show that his teaching on justification establishes rather than annuls the law, Paul turns in Romans 4 to the case of Abraham. Focusing on the text of Gen 15:6 ("Abraham believed God, and it was credited to him as righteousness"), as quoted in Rom 4:3, Paul argues that Abraham is the outstanding example of a person who was declared righteous by God on the basis of his trusting faith in God rather than on the basis of something he did or accomplished.

In the first half of the chapter (4:1-12), Paul focuses on the way that God credited righteousness (a status of being in a right covenant relation with God) to Abraham before he was circumcised. When he was not yet circumcised, Abraham was like any other uncircumcised Gentile. But because he believed and trusted in God's promise, God credited righteousness to Abraham on the basis of his trusting faith in God's promise. Thus Abraham was *justified* on the basis of trusting faith in God rather than on the basis of *doing* the works of the law. In the second half of this chapter, from which this text is drawn (4:13-25), Paul directs his attention to the nature of Abraham's faith. This is the point of entry for my homily, which seeks to explain what it means to believe.

The Homily

Introduction. Every week, after the gospel and homily, we profess our faith. With Christians throughout the world we profess our faith in God the Creator, Jesus our Redeemer, and the Holy Spirit who sanctifies us. But what does it mean to believe in God?

Exposition. For some, faith is an assent of the intellect: "I believe that God exists; I believe that Jesus Christ is his Son; I believe that the Holy Spirit is present and active in my life." All of this, of course, is true. But in today's second reading, taken from his great letter to the Romans, the Apostle Paul reminds us of another aspect of faith—faith is trust and confidence in the God who raises the dead.

For St. Paul, Abraham is the outstanding example of what it means to believe. For at the very moment in his life when there was no human reason to believe in God, Abraham trusted in God's promise.

The story of Abraham can be summarized in this way. Abraham and his wife Sarah were childless. Both of them were old, and there was no human possibility they would ever have a family. But at the very moment when Sarah was far beyond the age for bearing children, God promised Abraham that he would be the father of a great nation, that his offspring would be as numerous as the stars of the heaven, and that all the nations of the earth would find a blessing in his descendants.

What a marvelous promise! Abraham and Sarah would have numerous offspring; Abraham would be the father of a great nation. But how could this be? After all, Abraham was nearly a hundred years old, and his wife Sarah not far behind. How could God fulfill such a promise? What was Abraham to do? Should he trust in God's promise, or should he trust in his own common sense?

It is at this point that St. Paul writes, "hoping against hope," Abraham believed. He did not weaken in faith but was fully convinced that what God had promised, God was able to do. Although Abraham knew it was physically impossible for Sarah and him to have children, *he trusted* in God's promise; *he trusted* in the God who gives life to the dead and "calls into being what does not exist."

Abraham trusted in the power of God to do what he could not do. *Abraham trusted* in the power of God to bring life out of the dead womb of Sarah. *Abraham trusted* in the God who raises the dead.

The faith of Abraham, then, was not merely an intellectual assent to the truth; it was an act of total trust in the God who raises the dead. *The faith of Abraham* understood that nothing is impossible for God. *The faith of Abraham* was an act of obedience.

Application. *What does it mean to believe?* It means to trust in God when it appears that there is no reason to believe. *What does it mean to believe?* It means to trust in God when it appears that there is no reason to hope. *What does it mean to trust in God?* It means to trust that God is powerful to do what we cannot do.

Conclusion. As we celebrate this Eucharist, we trust in the God and Father of Jesus Christ, the God who raises the dead. As we eat the bread and drink the cup, we affirm our confidence that God can do what we cannot do. For we believe in the God who raises the dead.

After the Homily

The introduction to this homily is brief and without any self-reference. It simply reminds the congregation of what they do week after week, and it introduces a question that will become the central theme of the homily: what does it mean to believe in God? This question is central to Paul's exposition of Romans. It remains important for contemporary Christians, many of whom view faith as merely an intellectual assent to truth.

Whereas last week's homily began with a brief exposition of the text and concluded with a longer application, this week's homily begins with an extended exposition and concludes with a brief application. The reason for this is that the exposition of the text already invites the congregation to apply the text to themselves.

The exposition begins by stating that whereas some view faith as an intellectual assent, Paul reminds us of another aspect of faith: faith is trust in God who raises the dead.

In the exposition that follows I have tried to highlight the impossible dilemma in which Abraham and Sarah found themselves. On the one hand, God promised them a child who would be a source of blessing to the world. But on the other hand, the promise appears utterly foolish given their advanced age. The point of setting up this dilemma is to highlight faith as trust in God who is able to call into being what does not exist. Abraham's faith, then, was not merely an assent of the will; it was a trusting faith in the God who raises the dead. Abraham already believed in the God who would raise Jesus from the dead.

Toward the end of this homily I conclude with a rather brief application that is introduced by a series of questions that the congregation should be able to answer once they have heard the story of Abraham. Christian faith is the kind of faith that Abraham manifested when he trusted in God even though there was no human reason to trust in God apart from God's faithfulness. Accordingly, just as Abraham trusted in God because he believed that God was powerful to fulfill the promise, so Christians believe in God's promise of resurrection because they are confident that God will fulfill what God promised in his Son, Jesus Christ.

Like last week's homily, the latter part of this homily makes extensive use of repetition to reinforce its central point. I have indicated this repetition by the use of italics.

The homily ends with another brief conclusion that brings the congregation back to the liturgical act in which they are involved. It reminds the congregation that every time they celebrate the Eucharist, they affirm their faith in the God who raises the dead.

God's Proven Love for Us
Romans 5:6-11

Before the Homily

The reading for the eleventh Sunday is taken from the opening of Romans 5. According to my outline (pp. 8–10), chapter 5 marks the beginning of the third part of Romans: "The Experience of Salvation in the Light of God's Righteousness" (5:1–8:39). This is the great central section of Romans in which Paul describes the new situation in which the justified and reconciled find themselves: they are justified and at peace with God, for they are no longer enslaved to the cosmic powers of sin and death that once controlled their lives. Moreover, since they now live in the realm of God's life-giving Spirit, they are no longer under the regime of the Mosaic Law. Justified and reconciled to God, they have been transferred to the realm of the Spirit that empowers them to live in a way that is pleasing to God and that assures them they will be raised from the dead.

Since the Lectionary text from today's reading (Rom 5:6-11) is part of a larger unit (Rom 5:1-11), those who preach from this text should keep that larger unit in view, which sets the stage for what follows. In 5:1 Paul describes the new situation in which those who believe in Christ find themselves: they have been justified by faith, and now they are at peace with God. In saying that believers have been justified, the Apostle means that God has acquitted and declared them innocent. Consequently, believers are in a right covenant relationship with God because of what God has done for them in Christ rather than because of anything they have done. In writing that they are at peace with God, Paul means that they have been reconciled to God. Because of this new situation, believers can boast in their hope of the glory that will be theirs when they are raised from the dead. Furthermore, they can even boast of the afflictions they endure for the gospel.

Today's Lectionary reading makes two points: (1) God's love for us and (2) our assurance of final salvation. The proof of God's love for us is that Christ died for us when we were still alienated from God, when we were sinners, when we were without God. Precisely at that moment when we had no claim on God, God claimed us as his own through the saving death of his Son. This is how God justified, acquitted, and declared us innocent in his sight.

Having identified God's love for us with Christ's death for us, Paul asks two rhetorical questions that make the following points (5:9-10): First, if God justified us when we were alienated from him, then we can be all the more confident, now that we are justified, that we will be saved from the final judgment. Second, if God reconciled us when we were at enmity with him, now that we are reconciled to God we can be all the more confident of the final salvation that will be ours at the resurrection of the dead.

The homily that follows focuses on the assurance we have for final salvation because of God's proven love for us.

The Homily

Introduction. Everybody wants some assurance they are loved—perhaps a small sign of appreciation, some indication that they are loved and appreciated. And, of course, everybody wants some assurance about the future—a sense of security that, in the end, all will be well.

Exposition. This is why today's second reading, taken from St. Paul's great letter to the Romans, is so important for our lives. Reflecting and meditating on the significance of Christ's death, Paul draws an intimate relationship between the death of Christ and God's love for us. Observing that it is only with great difficulty that a person would die for another—even for a good person—Paul says that God proved his love for us in and through the death of his Son, Jesus Christ. At the very moment when we were most helpless and in need of God's grace, at the very moment when we were still sinners, Christ died for us. *Christ did not die for us when* we were good and just. *Christ did not die for us because* we were already in God's grace. *Christ died for us when* we were most in need.

Paul then goes on to say that since we now stand in a right relation to God because of Christ, we can be all the more confident about the future. *Because we* have already been reconciled to God, *we can be all the more confident* that God will save us from the powers of sin and death. *Because we* belong to Christ, *we can be confident* that we will not be separated from Christ or God at the moment of death.

Application. Human relations and our daily circumstances change. *At one time* in our lives we feel loved. *At another time* we feel abandoned and betrayed. *At one moment* all is well, and we feel confident about the future. *At another moment* everything appears so insecure, and we are filled with doubt and anxiety.

It is precisely at such moments that we need to return to what is truly important in our lives. It is at such moments that we need to recall the larger picture, the greater drama of which we are a part.

God's love for us is unconditional. In Christ, God manifested his love for us. We are not loved because of anything we have done or accomplished but because God loves us in and through his Son, Jesus Christ.

In the end, all will be well, not because of anything we have done or accomplished, but because God will complete the good work he has begun in Christ. *Now that we are in a right relationship with God,* we can be confident that God will save us. *Now that we are reconciled to God,* we can be confident that God will not abandon us.

Conclusion. As we celebrate this Eucharist, we give thanks for the assurance of love that we have in Christ, the assurance we have in Christ that all will be well.

After the Homily

The introduction to this homily is brief and to the point. Consisting of only two sentences, it reminds the congregation of the need human beings have to be loved and their deep-seated desire for security and assurance about the future. Although brief, the introduction sets up the body of the homily in which the focus will be on God's proven love for us, which is our assurance of final salvation.

Unlike my first two homilies, this homily manifests a balance between exposition and application. The exposition seeks to present what Paul writes without dwelling on the technical language of justification and reconciliation. Thus, instead of talking about being justified or reconciled, I have chosen to use the more familiar language of relationship because it communicates what Paul means by the language of justification. To be justified and reconciled to God is to be related to God in a new way that God brings about through the death of his Son.

The application of the homily begins with an experience that resonates with most people. At different moments in our lives, all of us feel betrayed and abandoned. On the basis of this experience, I call the congregation to recall God's unconditional love for us. Although we may be disappointed in our human relationships, we can be utterly confident of the relationship that God has established with us in and through the death of his Son. Employing Paul's own rhetoric, I then argue that if we are in a right relationship with God now, we can be all the more confident that God will save us.

The homily ends with another brief conclusion that reminds the congregation of the Eucharist they are about to receive and summarizes the main theme of the homily: our assurance in Christ of God's love, which is our assurance that all will be well.

The Origin of Sin
Romans 5:12-15

Before the Homily

Today's reading presents numerous challenges. It is complex and difficult to read, and perhaps even more difficult to understand when one hears it from the pew. Nevertheless, this is a theologically rich passage that stands at the heart of Paul's theology.

The text is part of a larger unit (5:12-21) that draws a comparison between Adam and Christ to explain why and how God justified and reconciled humanity to himself. Although the basic comparison is simple—whereas Adam's disobedience brought sin and death into the world, Christ's obedience brought grace and life into the world—the manner in which Paul presents this comparison is not. The basic problem is that Paul begins a comparison between Adam and Christ in 5:12 that he does not complete until 5:17-18. But when he does complete the comparison, the point he makes is clear: Adam and Christ are polar opposites. Whereas Adam, through his singular act of disobedience, was the progenitor of a history of sin and death, Christ has become the progenitor of a history of grace and life through his singular act of obedience.

This passage has played an important role in the church's teaching on original sin. Although the homily that follows does not refer to original sin, it deals with one of the major aspects of this doctrine: the continuing presence of sin in the world. The homily explains the presence of evil in the world in the light of the history of sin and death that Adam inaugurated by his singular transgression. It then calls upon the congregation to be in solidarity with the new Adam rather than with the old Adam.

The Homily

Introduction. Despite our best efforts, there is evil in the world. If you read the newspaper or watch the evening news, you will see and read tragic stories year in and year out. But why is there such evil? Why does evil persist in our world? More importantly, can this evil be overcome? Has this evil been overcome?

Exposition. In today's second reading, taken from his letter to the Romans, St. Paul provides us with an answer to these questions in his story of two men: (1) Adam, the first human being through whom sin and death entered the world; (2) Christ, the new human being whose saving death brought us grace and life.

The first human, Adam, began a history of sin and death when he rebelled against God. Seeking to be like God, Adam defiantly disobeyed the one who had given him life, and he rebelliously proclaimed that he could live apart from God. And so, St. Paul writes, "through one man sin entered the world, and through sin, death, and thus death came to all. . ." Ever since that moment, humanity has found itself trapped by its own desires and devices. Trapped by its desire to live apart from God, humanity finds itself in a predicament from which it cannot escape.

In the fullness of time, however, God sent his own Son, born of a virgin, a man like us in every way but sin, to do what we could not do. *Unlike Adam* who strove to be like God, *the Son of God* emptied himself to be like us. *Unlike Adam* who was disobedient to God, *the Son of God* was completely obedient to God. *Unlike Adam* who began a history of sin and death, *the Son of God* began a history of grace and life. And so St. Paul writes, "if by the transgression of the one many died, how much more did the grace of God and the gracious gift of the one man Jesus Christ overflow for the many."

Application. We live between two human beings: the old Adam who brings sin and death, and the new Adam who brings grace and life. Every day, then, we must choose to live in solidarity with one or the other. *We live in solidarity with the old Adam,* when, like Adam, we try to become like gods. *We live in solidarity with the old Adam* when, like Adam, we make ourselves the center of the universe. *We live in solidarity with the old Adam* when, like Adam, we forget the one who gave us life. Living in solidarity with Adam, we choose death rather than life.

But *when we live in solidarity with Christ*, we are part of a new creation in which grace and life abound. *When we live in solidarity with Christ*, the powers of sin and death are no longer at work in our lives. *When we live in solidarity with Christ*, we diminish the power of evil that Adam introduced in our world.

Conclusion. *In celebrating this Eucharist*, we choose to live in solidarity with Christ. *In celebrating this Eucharist*, we become part of a new creation of grace and life. *In celebrating this Eucharist*, we become one with Christ. Come, then, let us eat the bread and drink from the cup that brings us grace and life.

After the Homily

This brief introduction summarizes what nearly everyone observes: the continuing presence of evil in the world. Some secularists and humanists may be tempted to say that although humanity hasn't got it right yet, some day it will; believers understand (or at least they should understand) that the continuing presence of evil in the world is part of a mystery that Christianity has sought to explain in its teaching on original sin. The purpose of my brief introduction, then, is to call attention to the mystery of evil in order to provide the congregation with Paul's analysis of the human situation.

Given the complexity of Paul's Adam-Christ comparison, today's homily requires an especially clear and coherent exposition of what the Apostle is saying. Rather than reproduce Paul's argument in all its complexity, I have chosen to present the Pauline comparison in terms of two stories: the story of the first human being who began a history of sin and death, and the story of the new human being who began a history of grace and life. Given the nature of the homily, there is no need to get into the question of the historical existence of Adam. Instead, the focus should remain on the comparison that Paul draws between these two men: whereas one was disobedient with disastrous consequences for all who followed him, the other was obedient with salvific consequences for all who are incorporated into him.

Having summarized Paul's main point in this exposition, my application summons the congregation to live in solidarity with the new Adam rather than with the old Adam. To be sure, believers are already in solidarity with Christ inasmuch as they have been baptized into his saving death. But even though believers are *already* justified, they are *not yet* finally saved. Consequently, in this period between present justification and final salvation (which will occur at the general resurrection of the dead), they must continually reaffirm their solidarity with Christ rather than with Adam. Toward the end of this homily, I give several concrete examples of how believers live either in solidarity with Adam or in solidarity with Christ.

The homily ends with a brief conclusion that reminds the congregation that the Eucharist they are about to receive is the outstanding way in which they stand in solidarity with Christ, the new Adam.

Baptized into Christ's Death
Romans 6:3-4, 8-11

Before the Homily

Today's reading is taken from Romans 6, a chapter in which Paul explains why it is incongruous for Christians to persist in sin. The occasion for this chapter is a remark Paul makes at the end of the previous chapter: "where sin increased, grace overflowed all the more" (5:20). In light of that remark, Paul raises an objection to his gospel. If God's grace increased when we sinned, perhaps we should continue to sin so that God's grace will abound all the more (6:1). Today's reading is Paul's response to this objection.

In the first part of the reading (6:3-4) Paul reminds the Romans of the significance of their baptism. When they were baptized, they died to the power of sin over their lives by their participation in Christ's death. Whereas sin formerly ruled over their lives when they were in the old Adam, sin no longer rules over them now that they are in Christ, the new Adam. Dead to sin, they are free to serve God.

Notice the way in which Paul develops his argument in these verses. He says that at our baptism we were buried with Christ in his death so that as Christ was raised from the dead we might live "in newness of life" (6:4). Although we might have expected Paul to write that just as we were buried with Christ in his death so we were raised with Christ, this is not what the Apostle writes. Focusing on the ethical implications of baptism, he says that we died with Christ in baptism so that we might live *in newness of life*, by which Paul means a life empowered by God's Spirit. It is incongruous, then, for those who have died with Christ to persist in sinning.

In the second part of this reading (6:8-11) Paul reminds the Romans that if they have already died with Christ through their baptismal association with his death, they will live with him when they are raised from the dead. Baptismal participation in Christ's death, then, is the assurance of resurrection life. But if believers hope to participate in Christ's resurrection, they must live out the implication of their baptism: they must view themselves as dead to sin for the purpose of living in newness of life.

In the homily that follows I decided to pair this reading with the gospel (Matt 10:37-42) in which Jesus talks about the demands of discipleship. Thus the homily seeks to develop the theme of discipleship from two points of view: Jesus' call to take up the cross and follow him, and Paul's description of baptism as participation in Christ's death. Although Jesus and Paul describe the life of discipleship differently, both point to the need to pass through death in order to enter life.

The Homily

Introduction. The Christian life can be described in many ways. For example, the gospel we have just heard portrays the Christian life as a life of discipleship. Those who embrace this life must follow Jesus on the way. So Jesus says to his disciples, "whoever does not take up his cross and follow after me is not worthy of me."

Exposition. But in today's second reading St. Paul describes the Christian life as participation in Christ's death and resurrection. Christians are those who have died to sin through their baptism into Christ's death so that they can live in what St. Paul calls "newness of life," a life determined by the power of God's Spirit rather than by the power of sin.

This morning's liturgy, then, provides us with two ways to think of our Christian life: (1) as a life of discipleship and (2) as a life characterized by participation and sharing in the mystery of Christ's death and resurrection.

Application. We begin with the second image: the Christian life is a life of participation and sharing in the mystery of Christ's death and resurrection. Although we did not realize it at the time, we entered into the mystery of Christ's saving death at our baptism. Plunged into the waters of baptism, we died to an old way of life: a life of sin that led to death. And when we arose from the waters of baptism, we were born into newness of life: a life of grace that leads to eternal life.

What happened at our baptism is something we need to repeat every day of our life. *Every day of our life* we must die to our old self and rise with Christ to newness of life. *Every day of our life* we must die to sin and rise with Christ to newness of life. The Christian life, then, is a life of sharing and participation in the death and resurrection of Christ. Begun at our baptism into Christ's death, this newness of life will find its completion when we are raised from the dead.

Exposition. The second image is similar to the first. If we are to live the Christian life, we must be followers and learners of Jesus. *We must* study what Jesus did, *we must* learn what he said, and *we must* imitate him in our life. But *following Christ is never easy* because it inevitably leads to the cross. *Following Christ is never easy* because it leads to his death. This is why Jesus is so insistent in today's gospel that nothing, not even our own life, is more important than the life of discipleship. *If we try to save our life*, we will lose our life. *If we try to save our life* by refusing to take up our cross, we will not share Christ's resurrection life. It is only by surrendering our life and by entering into the mystery of Christ's death that we will gain our life at the resurrection of the dead.

Application. What does it mean to be a Christian? How should we live our Christian lives today? If we are to be Christians, we need to be followers of Christ, his disciples. And if we are to be his disciples, we must share in the mystery of his death and resurrection, both in the sacraments we celebrate and in the way in which we live our lives each day.

Conclusion. As we celebrate this Eucharist in which we proclaim the death of the Lord until he comes again, we ask for the grace to conform our lives to the mystery of his saving death and resurrection.

After the Homily

Although the Lectionary does not coordinate the Pauline readings with the gospel readings in the way that it coordinates the reading from the Old Testament with the gospel, there are times when it is helpful to draw a connection between the Pauline reading and the gospel. This is what I have done in this homily.

The homily begins with a simple introduction that highlights the main theme I wish to communicate: although the life of discipleship can be described in different ways, the essence of discipleship is participation in Jesus' suffering and death. For example, Jesus summons people to take up their cross and follow him, and Paul presents the Christian life as participation in Christ's death and resurrection.

This homily has two expositions and two applications, which show how the simple pattern of exposition followed by application can be altered. The first exposition deals with the Pauline text, the second with the gospel. In both instances, a brief application follows the exposition.

The first exposition focuses on an aspect of baptism that many contemporary Christians overlook: baptism is a participation in Christ's death and resurrection. This Pauline understanding of the sacrament needs to supplement the image of washing away sin that dominates the understanding of most believers. While there is biblical support for the image of washing away sin, the second image of dying with Christ is more powerful and lies at the heart of Paul's theology.

The second exposition deals with the text of the gospel. Here the focus is on Jesus' call to take up one's cross and follow him. These words will be familiar to many congregations, who are accustomed to thinking of the Christian life as following Jesus in the way of discipleship.

The unifying concept of this homily is found in the applications to both expositions. Although the Pauline reading speaks of baptism and the gospel speaks of discipleship, the point of unity between them is the need to pass through death in order to enter life. The gospel highlights this by proclaiming that believers must take up their cross and follow Jesus. Paul explains the life of discipleship as baptismal participation in Christ's death in order to live in newness of life.

The homily ends with a brief conclusion that reminds the congregation that the Eucharist they celebrate each week proclaims the death of the Lord until he comes. It then invites the congregation to pray for a deeper understanding of the mystery in which they participate each week.

The Spirit and the Flesh
Romans 8:9, 11-13

Before the Homily

With today's reading the Lectionary begins the first of five readings taken from Romans 8, which is Paul's most important statement about the role of the Spirit in the Christian life. Given the importance of Romans 8 for the Christian life, it will be helpful to preview this chapter before discussing today's second reading.

According to my outline (pp. 8–10), Romans 8 belongs to the third part of Paul's letter: "The Experience of Salvation in the Light of God's Righteousness" (Romans 5–8). In this part of Romans Paul describes the new situation of those who have been justified and reconciled to God by the obedience of Christ, the new Adam (Romans 5). In Christ, they are no longer slaves of sin and death (Romans 6). Moreover, because they belong to the realm of God's grace, they are no longer under a law frustrated by sin (Romans 7). Having explained the new freedom that the justified enjoy in Christ, the new Adam, in Romans 8 Paul describes the new life they live in the realm of God's Spirit.

The chapter consists of three sections. In the first, Paul portrays the Spirit as the source of the new life that believers enjoy (8:1-17). In the second, he presents the Spirit as the source of their hope (8:18-30). In the third, he assures them of God's irrevocable love for them (8:31-39). Today's reading belongs to the first of these three sections.

This text, however, presents two terms that can be confusing to the preacher as well as to the congregation: "the flesh" and "the Spirit." These terms are diametrically opposed to each other. The flesh is Paul's metaphor for all that is mortal and destined for death, by which Paul means eternal separation from God. It is not to be confused or identified with sexual desire, although inordinate sexual desire is a manifestation of living according to the flesh.

Rather, the flesh is a metaphor for a way of life that is opposed to God. It is the realm of sin and death; it is the realm in which Adam and the old humanity dwell.

In contrast to the flesh, the Spirit refers to the Spirit of God, the Holy Spirit. Unlike the flesh, the Spirit is immortal, the source of life. Those who live in the realm of the Spirit are in Christ, the new Adam. Although those who are in the Spirit will die (just as Christ died), the Spirit is their assurance of resurrection from the dead.

According to Pauline anthropology, human beings are either "in the flesh" or "in the Spirit." If they are in the flesh, they are still in the old Adam and so destined for death, which is eternal separation from God. But if they are in the Spirit, they are in Christ and destined for resurrection life.

The homily that follows explains this distinction and draws out its implication for the life of those who are in Christ.

The Homily

Introduction. Nothing is more important than knowing who we are. *If we know who we are*, we are at peace with ourselves, and we can be at peace with each other. *If we know who we are*, we know what we must do and how to act. *If we know who we are*, we begin to understand something of our future and our destiny.

Exposition. A good example of what I mean can be found in today's second reading, which is taken from St. Paul's letter to the Romans. In this letter, from which we have been reading for the past several weeks, the Apostle reminds us of the salvation that God has graciously and freely extended to us in Jesus Christ. In doing so Paul has provided us with a reliable understanding of who we are in Christ.

For example, *we have learned* that we have been reconciled to God through the death of his Son. *We have learned* that we belong to Christ who is the new Adam, the obedient Son of God. *We have learned* that so long as we belong to Christ, the powers of sin and death can no longer control and threaten our lives.

In today's reading from Romans, Paul provides us with a further insight to our new identity in Christ when he writes: "You are not in the flesh; on the contrary, you are in the spirit, if only the

Spirit of God dwells in you." In saying that we are not in the flesh, Paul means that we no longer belong to the realm of sin and death. We belong to the realm of God's Spirit. By the realm of the Spirit, Paul means all that is immortal, incorruptible, and so destined for unending life. *To be sure*, we still live in the world. *To be sure*, we still face suffering and death. *To be sure*, we have not yet reached the final goal of our life. But something has changed. Something is different. *Whereas formerly* our lives were under the power of sin, this is no longer the case. *Whereas formerly* our lives were threatened by eternal separation from God, this is no longer the case. Living in the realm of God's Spirit, the power of God's Spirit is at work in us. *The power of God's Spirit* enables us to do what we formerly could not do. *The power of God's Spirit* assures us of new and lasting life.

Application. Consider for a moment what a difference it makes in our lives when we dwell in the realm of the Spirit rather than in the realm of the flesh. *If we live our lives* according to the power of God's Spirit, then the Spirit will empower us to do God's will. *If we live our lives* according to the power of God's Spirit, then we are assured of new and resurrection life. *If we live our lives* according to the power of God's Spirit, we will live as sisters and brothers of Christ.

Living according to the Spirit does not require us to flee or escape from the world. *Those who live according to the Spirit* continue to live in the world and enjoy the good things of this life. *Those who live according to the Spirit* continue to celebrate the wonder and glory of creation. *Those who live according to the Spirit* continue to work for the good and betterment of society. But *in doing so,* they do all things in Christ. *In doing so,* they celebrate the glory of God that changes and transforms their live. Those who live in the Spirit, however, understand that there is more to life than what they see, what they hear, and what they touch. They know that life is full of the mystery that is God. And so they live in the world with the confidence that all has been changed and transformed by God's grace.

Conclusion. In celebrating the Eucharist each week, we proclaim that we belong to the realm of the Spirit. In celebrating the Eucharist, we are united with Christ and the Spirit of God. In celebrating the Eucharist, we affirm that we no longer live our lives according to the flesh. As we eat the bread and drink from the cup, then, we ask for the grace to live our lives in the Spirit.

After the Homily

I begin this homily by drawing attention to the relationship between who we are and how we act. While most of us recognize that what we do reveals who we are, we do not always consider that who we are determines what we do. This relationship is especially true in Pauline theology, which affirms that the new being we have become in Christ enables and empowers us to live in a new way.

Having introduced my main theme, I begin the exposition by reminding the congregation what we have learned about our Christian identity from Paul's letter to the Romans: our identity is grounded and rooted in Christ, the new Adam. This is why we are called Christians. After reminding the congregation of their fundamental identity in Christ, I turn my attention to today's reading in which Paul describes this identity in terms of being in the Spirit rather than being in the flesh. Here the challenge is to communicate an understanding of spirit and flesh that is not equated with soul and body. I want the congregation to understand that the expressions "in the Spirit" and "in the flesh" refer to two different realms, two opposing ways of life. Thus the embodied self is either "in the Spirit" or "in the flesh," depending on a person's basic orientation in life. Those who commit themselves only to what they can see, hear, and touch are in the flesh, whereas those who commit themselves to the gospel God has revealed in Christ are in the Spirit.

Having summarized what Paul means by these two terms, I have tried to apply them to the life of the congregation. But instead of focusing on both terms, I decided to highlight the expression "living in the Spirit" since it summarizes Paul's understanding of the Christian. Here, I tried to dispel any notion that living in the Spirit means separation or disengagement from the material world. The "spiritual" person is fully engaged in the material world. This engagement, however, occurs in light of the gospel and under the power and influence of God's grace.

The purpose of the conclusion, which reminds the congregation of the Eucharist they are about to celebrate, is to relate "being in the Spirit" with receiving the Eucharist. Those who participate in the Eucharist are in the Spirit. Accordingly, to live one's life in light of the Eucharist that one receives is to live according to the Spirit.

The Fullness of Salvation
Romans 8:18-23

Before the Homily

This reading challenges believers to broaden their understanding of the salvation God has in store for them. Whereas many contemporary Christians think of salvation in terms of saving their soul, Paul's vision is more expansive. The salvation God has effected in Christ embraces our body as well as our soul, the whole of God's creation as well as humankind.

The reading begins with a simple statement of Paul's faith and trust in the salvation God has in store for the justified: there is no comparison between the sufferings that we presently endure for the sake of the gospel and the glory that is to be revealed.

The word "glory" appears several times in Romans. Sometimes Paul applies it to God; other times he applies it to human beings. In this instance, it refers to the glory that the justified will enjoy at the resurrection of the dead when they will be glorified just as Christ was gloried when God raised him from the dead. There is no comparison, then, between that glory and the sufferings of the present time.

After this opening statement, Paul personifies inanimate creation and says that creation itself is waiting for the moment when the justified and redeemed will attain this resurrection glory. This is a remarkable statement. Treating creation as if it were a living, thinking organism, Paul presents it as anticipating the moment when redeemed humanity will enjoy the glory for which God destined it. At that moment, creation itself will be set free from the futility to which God subjected it. Here, Paul is alluding to Adam's transgression that alienated humanity from God, thereby frustrating the purpose of creation. This is why creation is groaning and longing for our glorification, which will occur with "the redemption of our bodies" (8:23), by which Paul means our resurrection from the dead.

In preaching from this text, I have sought to broaden the way in which the congregation thinks about salvation. My goal is two-fold. First, I want to remind believers that we will be saved body and soul. It is not a part of us but the whole of us that will be saved. Second, I have tried to highlight the cosmic dimension of salvation. In a way known only to God, the whole of creation will be involved in salvation. Nothing will be lost.

The Homily

Introduction. Every generation, including our own, faces difficult times, periods when it appears that daily life is becoming more difficult, times when it seems that the best days are behind us, moments when we wonder what is happening to the world we knew.

Exposition. St. Paul faced such moments in his own life and ministry. But in today's second reading, taken from his letter to the Romans, he looks at the present in light of the future that God has prepared for the whole of creation as well as for the redeemed. Filled with faith and hope in the God who redeemed us by the blood of his Son, St. Paul says that the sufferings of the present are as nothing when compared with the glory that will be revealed in us. The glory of which St. Paul speaks is the glory that we will enjoy at the resurrection of the dead. *At that moment* we shall be like the risen Lord, glorified and transformed. *At that moment* death will have no power over us. *At that moment* we will share in the very glory and life of God. *At that moment* the sufferings that we presently endure will seem small and insignificant.

St. Paul's vision of the future that God has in store for us, however, does not end with our salvation. Looking to the created world about him, the great apostle says that when we have been set free from sin and death, creation itself will also be set free from the slavery to corruption that presently frustrates it. Put another way, for St. Paul the salvation that God has in store for us is greater than we can imagine. It is not merely the salvation of our souls that is at stake; it is the salvation of our bodies and the entire cre-ated world in which we live. We will be saved body as well as soul and, when we are, the whole of creation will be redeemed as well.

I suppose we could say that St. Paul, who understood the goodness of God's creation, was an environmentalist before his time. But more than any environmentalist, he envisioned a creation changed and transformed by the power of God's grace—a creation transfigured by the glory of God, a creation born anew.

Application. As Christians, we live between two worlds: the present world that we see about us and the world that is yet to be born, God's new creation. On the one hand, we live in a world where suffering and pain will always be present; for the world in which we live is subject to death and decay. But on the other hand, we live in hope of another world into which the risen Lord Jesus Christ has already entered. We live in hope of entering God's new creation. *Although we have not yet entered that new creation*, we already experience something of it each time we receive the Eucharist. *Although we have not yet entered that world*, we already experience something of it through the Spirit of Christ that dwells in us.

Conclusion. As we eat this bread and drink from this cup of the Eucharist, we ask for the grace to persevere in hope of the glory to be revealed; for the sufferings of the present are as nothing when compared with the glory to be revealed for us.

After the Homily

This homily begins with a brief introduction: a single sentence. Although brief, the introduction serves its purpose by summarizing a common experience. The present situation always seems dire. And so it appears that humanity is regressing rather than progressing. Such an attitude, however, is not the way that Christian faith understands its circumstances.

The exposition of the homily is longer than in other homilies because the Pauline concepts of this reading will not be familiar to most congregations. In the first part of the exposition I have tried to explain that the future glory Paul has in view is the glory that will be ours at the general resurrection of the dead. In the second part I turn my attention to the redemption of creation.

While the congregation confesses its faith in the general resurrection of the dead every week, this is a neglected article of the Creed that needs to be preached more often. The salvation we will enjoy is the same salvation that Jesus already enjoys: resurrection from the dead. At that moment death will be defeated once and for all, and it will no longer have any power over us.

Paul's teaching on the redemption of all creation broadens our understanding of salvation by reminding us that there is an intimate relationship between humankind and the created world. What Paul writes will indeed resonate with humanity's contemporary concern and care for the environment, but it should not be confused with it. What Paul has in view is greater than care for the environment. Paul is speaking about the redemption of creation.

The homily seeks to provide the congregation with reason to hope. The world that they see is not the whole of reality. There is a vision of the world that is only accessible to faith and hope. As is my usual practice, the homily concludes with a brief statement that focuses on the Eucharist.

Discerning the Mystery
Romans 8:26-27

Before the Homily

In last week's reading Paul spoke of creation groaning as it waits for the final salvation of humanity (8:22) and of the justified groaning for that moment when their bodies will be redeemed at the resurrection of the dead (8:23). Today's reading completes the theme of groaning by highlighting the "inexpressible groanings" of God's Spirit on behalf of the justified.

The groaning of the Spirit, however, does not refer to a longing or desire on the part of the Spirit for something (as it does in the case of creation and the justified) but to the intercession of the Spirit on behalf of the justified. Thus Paul presents the Spirit as one who intercedes on behalf of the justified much as the Fourth Evangelist presents the Spirit as the Paraclete or Advocate who defends the disciples and reminds them of all that Jesus said and did.

The Spirit intercedes with God (whom Paul calls "the one who searches hearts") on behalf of the justified with "inexpressible groanings." The groanings of the Spirit cannot be expressed in human words because the Spirit communicates with God who is mysterious and beyond all human comprehension.

The purpose of the Spirit's intercession is to assist the justified in their prayer and "groaning" for final redemption. This assistance is necessary because of "our weakness," by which Paul means our inability to discern the full plan of God. Consequently, although the justified pray, they need the assistance of the Spirit if they hope to pray in a way that accords with God's economy of salvation.

Although this brief reading may be puzzling to many, it makes an important point about prayer and our relationship to God: left to ourselves our prayer will always be inadequate because we do not know the mystery of God. Consequently, we pray in and through the power of God's Spirit who enlightens our understanding and strengthens our prayer by interceding on our behalf. It is the Spirit, then, that enables us to pray as we ought.

This is not an easy text from which to preach. But it is an opportunity to instruct the congregation about the Christian understanding of prayer in and with the Spirit. In the homily that follows I have paired this text with the gospel text by making the mystery of God my central theme.

The Homily

Introduction. The world in which we live is filled with mystery: the mystery of life and death, the mystery of love and hate, the mystery of God. For example, in today's gospel Jesus speaks in parables and reveals the mystery of God's plan for the world and for the church. He reveals that at the present time God allows good and evil to coexist in the world, and even in the church. But at the end of the ages, there will be a final reckoning, a moment when all that is good will be gathered into God's heavenly kingdom and all that is evil will be eternally destroyed.

Exposition. But if we live in a world filled with such mystery, *how can we know what we ought to do? How can we know how we ought to live?* St. Paul provides us with an answer to these questions in today's second reading taken from his letter to the Romans. Aware that left to ourselves we cannot comprehend the mystery of God's plan for our salvation, Paul assures us that the Spirit of God, the Holy Spirit, comes to the aid of our weakness. Because we do not know how to pray as we ought to pray, the Spirit of God intercedes for us.

The Spirit of God comes to the aid of our weakness. With these words St. Paul assures us that the Holy Spirit enables us to do what we cannot do by ourselves. *Left to ourselves,* we could never understand the mystery of God that has been revealed in the crucified Christ. *Left to ourselves,* we could never comprehend our profound need for God's grace and redemption. *Left to ourselves,* we could never understand the mysterious ways of God in our lives. This is why the Spirit of God comes to the aid of our weakness, enabling us to see and to hear, to understand and to comprehend the hidden mystery of God.

The Spirit of God intercedes for us. With these words Paul assures us that even though we are not aware of it, the Holy Spirit constantly makes intercession for us before God. Thus, *although we may not know how to pray* as we ought to pray, God's Spirit prays with and for us. *Although we may not know how to pray*, God's Spirit intercedes for our good. *Although we are not even aware of it*, the Holy Spirit is our constant intercessor, the one who pleads our cause.

Application. *Although we are not aware of it*, we live in a world filled with the mystery and grace of God, a world in which God's plan for our salvation is always at work, a world in which God's own Spirit is always present in our lives. *It is this world of mystery and grace* that will endure. *It is this world of mystery and grace* that will finally overcome the evil that is present in the world. *It is this world of mystery and grace* that will bring us salvation.

Conclusion. *By celebrating this Eucharist*, we enter into that mystery of the Lord's passion, death, and resurrection. *In celebrating this Eucharist*, we participate in the mystery of Christ's death and resurrection. And so *we are confident that* if we die with him, we will rise with him. *We are confident that* the mystery of God's grace will conquer and endure.

After the Homily

One of the difficult aspects of preaching from the second reading is that the congregation has just heard the gospel. This presents a challenge for preaching from Romans, which always occurs during the year of Matthew. For example, on this particular Sunday the congregation will have just heard Jesus' parable about the man who sowed good seed only to find weeds among the crop. Having just proclaimed this rather lengthy parable, it is not easy to move into such a short Pauline text. I have tried to overcome this difficulty by making the gospel for this week the introduction to my homily. To do this I have focused on the theme of mystery that characterizes Matthew's understanding of Jesus' parables. Matthew presents Jesus' parables as the fulfillment of a scriptural promise: "I will open my mouth in parables, I will announce what has lain hidden from the foundation of the world" (Matt 13:35).

This theme of "mystery" is worth pursuing because the Christian life is the mystery of God's economy (plan) for our redemption. Moreover, the Eucharist that the Christian assembly celebrates each week is a mystery inasmuch as it is a sacramental participation in their Lord's death and resurrection. For most people in the pew, however, a mystery is just another problem to be solved. There is little sense that life is filled with mystery that ought to evoke a sense of wonder and awe. There is an inadequate understanding of the Christian life as a mystery into which we are summoned to enter and live with the Lord.

My point of entry into today's homily, then, is the mystery of life, which is manifested in different ways. Having introduced the homily in this manner, I have raised the question of our relationship to the mystery of God that surrounds us. This has allowed me to speak about the reading from Romans in terms of discerning the mystery of God. It is the Holy Spirit, the Spirit of God, who enables us to discern how we can live in accordance with the mystery of God's plan for our salvation.

This particular homily makes use of repetition several times in order to reinforce its point. In the second paragraph it twice asks, "how can we know what we ought to do?" In the third paragraph it repeats the expression "left to ourselves" several times. In the fourth paragraph it repeats "although we may not" three times. I also use repetition in the conclusion.

Repetition is one of the most powerful rhetorical devices preachers have to communicate their message. Although the congregation will quickly forget the particulars of any homily, they will remember those phrases that repeat the main points. Here, my repetition hammers home that left to ourselves we do not know how we ought to live. But although we may not know how we ought to pray, the Spirit comes to our assistance.

The application of this particular homily also makes its point by repetition. We live in a world of mystery in which God is always at work, even when we are not aware of God's presence. The conclusion brings the congregation back to the Eucharist, which is the central mystery of the Christian life.

All Will Be Well
Romans 8:28-30

Before the Homily

Today's liturgy presents us with another short reading from Romans 8, the chapter we have been reading from for the past three weeks and will read again next week. The reading comes toward the end of the chapter. Having spoken in last week's reading of the Spirit's intercession that enables us to pray as we ought, Paul presents us in this week's reading with the full sweep of God's plan that can be outlined in this way: God foreknew, God predestined, God called, God justified, God glorified.

The statement that God predestined will cause difficulty for those who construe it in terms of double predestination: God has predestined some for heaven and others for hell. But this is not what Paul is talking about in this text or (in my view) any other text. It will be helpful then to summarize what the Apostle means by each phrase.

God foreknew. The divine economy of salvation begins with God's knowledge of those who will be justified. Those who have been justified, then, can be confident that they are involved in a drama of salvation. Their justification is not the result of random chance; it belongs to a plan grounded in God's knowledge.

God predestined. Because God foreknew them, God determined that they would be conformed to the image of his Son. Accordingly, just as God raised Jesus from the dead, so God predestined the justified to be raised from the dead.

God called. Because the justified have been predestined for resurrection life, God has called or elected them. Their new status in Christ, then, is not something they have determined for themselves but something God has determined for them. Accordingly, the Christian life is a vocation in the fullest sense of the term.

God justified. Those whom God called, God acquitted. That is, God declared them innocent on the basis of Jesus' saving death and resurrection. Accordingly, they now stand in a correct and proper relation to God.

God glorified. Although the fullness of glorification will only occur at the general resurrection of the dead when the mortal earthly body will be transformed into an immortal resurrection body by the power of God's life-giving Spirit, the justified are already glorified inasmuch as they possess the Spirit, the firstfruits of resurrection life.

If we look at God's divine plan from the point of view of the justified, this divine economy assures them of their role in God's salvific plan and of their final destiny, which is their glorification with Christ. It also proclaims to those who have not yet embraced the gospel that they will find their role in this divine economy when they enter into Christ, the new Adam.

Rather than take on the difficult question of predestination, I have chosen to focus on the assurance that this divine economy holds for those who are in Christ. If this is truly the situation of the justified, there is no room for worry and anxiety in the Christian life.

The Homily

Introduction. Nearly every day we find ourselves beset by worries and anxieties. Are my children safe? How will I care for my aging parents? Is my job secure? Will I have enough money to retire? But suppose someone could assure you that in the end everything will be all right, that your worries and anxieties are useless because all will be well. *If you could hear such a word* of comfort and assurance, would not your life be changed? *If you could hear such a word,* would you not live in a completely new way? *If you could hear such a word,* would it not be a moment of grace and relief that would set you free to live as you ought to live?

Exposition. This is precisely the kind of word that we have just heard in today's second reading in which St. Paul makes the bold claim "that all things work for good for those who love God." Supremely confident in God's purpose for creation, Paul trusts that God will not, God cannot, abandon those who trust in him. Indeed, because of what God has already done in his Son, Jesus Christ, St. Paul goes further. He is convinced that God, who knew us before we were born, predestined us to be glorified like his Son. So God called and justified us—that is, God forgave our sins.

Paul, of course, was hardly oblivious to the hardships of life. His own life was filled with sufferings and hardships, trials and afflictions that would have made most people despair. But in light of what God had already done in Jesus Christ, Paul understood God's purpose—that in the end all things will be well. Paul believed that God who called and justified us will also conform us to the glorious image of his Son, Jesus Christ.

Application. In the end, all things will be well. *When we have* passed through our trials and afflictions, we will look back and realize that all things work for good for those who love God. *When we have* endured our own sufferings and hardships, we will finally understand that our worries and anxieties were for naught because God was always caring and watching over us—for everything is for God's purpose. *When we have* finally completed our life's journey we will look back and ask, why did I worry so much? Why was I so anxious when the God and Father of Jesus Christ was always caring for me?

Conclusion. After reciting the Lord's Prayer, the priest recites a prayer in which he asks, "Deliver us, Lord, from every evil, and grant us peace in our day. In your mercy keep us free from sin and protect us from all anxiety as we wait in joyful hope for the coming of our Savior, Jesus Christ." May the Lord deliver us from all anxiety, for in the end, all things will be well for those who love God.

After the Homily

This homily begins with a longer than usual introduction that focuses on one of the most distinctive aspects of human experiences: worry and anxiety. An extended description of this experience, to which nearly everyone can relate, prepares for the body of the homily in which I argue that anxiety and worry are incongruous with the Christian life.

The exposition of the homily begins with a consideration of the phrase "all things work for good for those who love God"

(8:28). It then proceeds to explain why Paul could make such a statement. In light of what God had so recently done in his Son, Paul understood the divine economy of salvation. Given this new knowledge, Paul realized that all things will eventually work out for God's elect, despite the present tribulation.

Lest I present Paul as naively optimistic, in the third paragraph I remind the congregation of the many hardships that he endured. If anyone had a right to worry and be anxious, it was Paul. Nevertheless, despite all that he suffered in his ministry, and despite the many setbacks to his ministry, he was confident that all things would be well because everything is a part of God's economy for salvation.

In the application I invite the congregation to look at their lives from the perspective of God's divine economy. When we have finally arrived at our destination, we will understand all the twists and turns in our journey. Again, this is an experience to which most of us can easily relate. We are anxious and apprehensive at the beginning of a long journey, but when it is completed we look back and ask why we worried.

The conclusion makes use of the prayer that follows the Lord's Prayer, when the priest prays that the Lord will protect the community from all anxiety. In this way I seek to relate the text of Romans to the Eucharist the congregation is about to receive. Anxiety is incongruous with the Christian life for those who understand their place in the divine economy.

Forever United with Christ
Romans 8:35, 37-39

Before the Homily

With today's text we come to the Lectionary's final selection from Romans 8, from which we have been reading for the past five weeks. This particular text is also the climax of the first eight chapters of Romans in which Paul has presented his teaching on God's righteousness and our justification on the basis of God's saving grace through trusting faith in Jesus Christ. The Lectionary reading, however, is part of a larger unit from which several verses have been omitted. Accordingly, preachers should read the entire passage (8:31-39).

The central point of the reading is clear: there is nothing that can separate the justified from the love that God and Christ have for them. Paul makes this point immediately after his summary of the divine economy that he described in last week's reading. In that text, you will recall, the Apostle drew out, in bold strokes, the divine plan that began with God's foreknowledge and concluded with the glorification of the justified.

Today's reading draws out the logical consequences of this divine economy. If believers have been called and justified by God in order to be conformed to the image of the Son and so glorified, then there is nothing that can separate the justified from the love that God manifested for them through the death of his Son. God's eternal plan of salvation for the justified provides them with all the assurance they need that nothing can separate them from God's love.

This text is a tour de force. By simply asking a series of rhetorical questions that he then answers, Paul assures his readers of God's love for them. Homilists might try to imitate something of Paul's rhetoric to assure their own congregations that nothing can separate them from God's love for them. In doing so they will provide believers with a reason to live their lives with similar confidence and assurance.

The Homily

Introduction. The most fearful aspect of death is not the act of dying but the fear of being forever separated from those we love. *We will no longer* see their faces, *we will no longer* hear their voices, *we will no longer* touch them again. And so we are afraid.

Exposition. St. Paul experienced such moments of fear in his life. For example, in his second letter to the Corinthians he lists the many hardships that he suffered for the sake of Christ, noting that he was in danger of death again and again. Yet despite his fear of death, he trusted and believed that nothing, not even death, could separate him from Christ. And so he asks in today's second reading, "who will separate us from the love of Christ?"

The answer, of course, is that nothing can separate us from Christ, not even death, because Christ has overcome our death through his death and resurrection. But if nothing can separate us from Christ, then death cannot separate us from each other, so long as we remain in Christ. *In Christ,* we are one. *In Christ,* we are united to each other. *In Christ,* death has been defeated. So long as we are in Christ, nothing can separate us from Christ or from each other—not even death itself.

Application. Consider the power that we have in our faith. Throughout our lives, there are moments of discouragement and disappointment, moments of sickness and failure, moments when it appears that all that we love and have is about to collapse. At such times we may feel alone and isolated, fearful that we will be separated from those we love. But it is precisely at such moments that faith overcomes fear. For *if we truly believe that we are in Christ*, nothing can separate us from Christ. And *if we truly believe that we are in Christ*, nothing can separate us from each other.

Our lives can be changed and transformed by the simple knowledge and the trusting faith that we are in Christ. *Our lives can be renewed* by the profound realization that, when we receive this Eucharist, we are in Christ and Christ is in us. And if Christ is in us, and we are in Christ, nothing can separate us from Christ or from each other.

Conclusion. In today's first reading the prophet Isaiah invites us to come to the water, to eat and drink without cost. This living water is Christ. This water is the Eucharist that Christ gives us freely and without cost. We are like the crowds in today's gospel, whom Christ freely fed without cost. *Each time* we participate in this Eucharist, Christ feeds us with the gift of himself. *Each time* we share in that gift, we are one in Christ and one with each other. And because we are one in Christ, nothing can separate us from the love of God.

After the Homily

The homily begins with a brief introduction that focuses on the most universal of experiences: the fear of death. In doing so it suggests that the most fearful aspect of death is not the act of dying but the separation from those we know and love. This simple example provides the foundation for the rest of the homily that proclaims that neither death nor anything else can separate those who are in Christ from each other since Christ has overcome the power of death by rising from the dead.

The exposition begins with an example from Paul's own life as illustrated in 2 Corinthians. Paul was constantly in danger of death throughout his ministry as he testifies in 2 Cor 11:22–12:10. Despite his many hardships and brushes with death, the Apostle maintained a sense of supreme confidence that not even death, the last and greatest enemy, could separate him from Christ.

On the basis of this brief exposition, I have applied this text to the life of the faithful. Like Paul, we experience moments of discouragement and disappointment, but there is a power to our faith, which is found in the simple phrase "in Christ." If we are "in Christ," then we are in the one who has overcome death. And if we are in the one who has overcome death, then death is no longer our master. To be sure, we will die, just as Christ died. But the gift of the Spirit (which has been the subject of Romans 8) is our assurance that just as God raised Christ from the dead, so God will raise us from the dead.

The conclusion to this homily is longer than most of my other conclusions. Moreover, in this particular conclusion I have made use of material from the first reading and the gospel of the day. In doing so I have tried to bring the congregation back to the Eucharist. Here I note that each time we participate in the Eucharist, we are in Christ in a unique way. And if we are in Christ, then nothing can separate us from the love that God and Christ have for us.

Paul's Love for His People
Romans 9:1-5

Before the Homily

The readings for the next three weeks will be drawn from the fourth part of Romans, which I have titled "God's Righteousness and the Destiny of Israel" (9:1–11:36). Although this part of Romans is not as familiar to most homilists and congregations as the first eight chapters of the letter, it plays a crucial role in Paul's discussion of God's righteousness. Having argued that God manifested his saving righteousness in Christ's death and resurrection, in this part of the letter Paul addresses the question of Israel's failure to embrace the gospel that proclaims this saving righteousness. The question that Paul raises here is of the utmost importance since it concerns God's faithfulness and reliability. Has Israel failed in its faithfulness to God, or has God failed to be faithful to Israel?

The response Paul gives to this question can be summarized in this way: It is not God who has been unfaithful but Israel that has failed to accept God's saving righteousness. God's ways have not changed, for God has always worked on the basis of election. Nevertheless, Israel's disobedience has played an important role in God's economy of salvation inasmuch as the Gentiles have embraced the gospel that Israel has rejected. God, however, has not repudiated Israel, as Paul will affirm in next week's reading. Therefore, in God's time, and in God's way, all Israel will be saved.

Today's reading provides us with a statement of Paul's love for his people that should dispel any notion that Paul was a Jewish apostate. Although the majority of his Jewish contemporaries did not accept Jesus as God's Messiah, Paul remains loyal to his people. How could it be otherwise? Israel was the beneficiary of the gifts that Paul lists toward the end of this reading: Israel is God's son;

God's glory dwelt in the temple; God made covenants with Abraham, Moses, and David; Israel received the law and instructions for worship at Mount Sinai and is the beneficiary of the promises God made to Abraham, Isaac, and Jacob. Most importantly, the Messiah comes from the people of Israel. These are, and these *remain*, Israel's privileges.

The homily that follows seeks to impress upon the congregation the love that Paul continues to have for his people and that Christians should have for the Jewish people today.

The Homily

Introduction. Throughout this summer, most of my homilies have dealt with some aspect of Paul's great letter to the Romans. This letter deserves our attention for several reasons. For example, it is Paul's most important statement about the gospel he preaches, and it provides us with a profound understanding of the salvation we have received in Jesus Christ. To use Paul's own terms, God has justified or acquitted us from sin; God has reconciled us to himself; God has given us the gift of the Spirit, which is our assurance of resurrection. But in today's reading Paul begins a new section of this letter in which he must deal with the failure of his people—the people of Israel, the Jewish people—to embrace the gospel he preaches. Given the ever-present danger of anti-Semitism, what Paul says here is of immense importance for our understanding of the Christian life.

Exposition. Paul begins today's reading with a personal statement in which he affirms his continuing love for his people. Filled with sorrow and anguish because the majority of them have not embraced the gospel, Paul goes so far as to say that he would be willing to be separated from God if this separation could bring his people to faith in Christ. Put another way, Paul is willing to sacrifice all that is precious and dear to him for the sake of his people.

The Apostle than goes on to list the privileges that God bestowed on the Jewish people: First, God called Israel his beloved son. Accordingly, all the people of Israel are God's sons and daughters. Second, the glory of God dwelt in their midst, especially in the temple. Third, they were the recipients of the Law of Moses, which enabled them to know God's will. Fourth, they enjoyed the worship of the temple. Fifth, they were the beneficiaries of God's promises and blessings. Sixth, Abraham, Isaac, and Jacob were their ancestors. Seventh, and most importantly, the Messiah came from the Jewish people.

It is little wonder, then, that Paul is so concerned for his people. If they have received so many privileges from God, why have they failed to embrace the gospel? What will their future be? As we will see next week, Paul is quite insistent that God has not rejected the Jewish people, and he is filled with hope and confidence that in God's own way, and in God's own time, Israel will be saved.

Application. Despite Paul's affirmation of love for his people and their central role in the drama of salvation, there has been a tragic history of anti-Judaism and anti-Semitism in Christianity. These sentiments of anti-Judaism and anti-Semitism can be summarized in this way: The Jewish people rejected Jesus as the Messiah and put him to death; therefore, God rejected them, and they are no longer God's people. This view, which is erroneous, becomes an excuse for people to treat the Jewish people with hatred and contempt. This anti-Semitism came to its climax in Nazi Germany during the Second World War when six million Jews were systematically put to death for the simple reason that they were Jews.

Although some have used the New Testament to justify their anti-Jewish sentiments, what St. Paul writes in today's reading, and what he will say in next week's reading, should dispel any notion that God has rejected the Jewish people as his people. In his letter to the Romans, especially in chapters 9–11, Paul is insistent that God has not rejected his people. *Paul is quite insistent* that God remains faithful to Israel. *Paul is quite insistent* that the Jewish people remain the people of God. *Paul is quite insistent* that in God's way, in God's time, in a way unknown to us, God will save his people.

Conclusion. Every time we celebrate this Eucharist, we are proclaiming the death of Jesus, the *Jewish* Messiah. Our faith, then, is intimately woven with the faith of Israel. How foolish it would be, then, for Christians to engage in any form of anti-Semitism. As we celebrate this Eucharist, we pray for the good of the Jewish people from whom Paul and the *Jewish* Messiah came forth. We pray for the good of the Jewish people whose faith is at the origin of our faith.

After the Homily

This is a difficult homily to preach for two reasons. First, few people believe or would acknowledge that they are anti-Semitic or that they harbor anti-Jewish sentiments. Moreover, if they harbor such feelings, they tend to rationalize their behavior by pointing to a particular Jewish person whose behavior, in their view, justifies such sentiments. Second, it is often difficult to maintain a distinction between the modern Jewish state of Israel, which is a political entity, and the Jewish people as a religious community. Consequently, when contemporary Christians hear the word "Israel" spoken from the pulpit, some may think of the state of Israel, whereas the preacher has in view the biblical people of Israel. For these reasons, I have found it necessary to be more didactic in this homily.

The introduction reviews what I have been preaching about this summer in order to prepare the congregation for today's reading in which the letter embarks upon a new topic that is unfamiliar to most congregations. Whereas Paul has been discussing God's salvific work in Christ, he now turns his attention to Israel. Consequently, it is important to prepare the congregation for this new topic.

In the exposition that follows I have given a brief commentary on the text. Here I have tried to do two things. First, and most importantly, I want to highlight Paul's anguish over the failure of his people to embrace the gospel in order to disabuse the congregation of any notion that Paul the Christian abandoned his people. Second, I have spent some time explaining each of Israel's privileges because I want the congregation to be aware of the important role that Israel has played in God's economy of salvation. Here it is important to highlight that Jesus is the *Jewish* Messiah.

The application of this homily is the crucial moment. How do we move from exposition to application? While many Christians rightly abhor anti-Semitism, they are not aware of the tragic role that it has played in this history of Christianity. Here, I have chosen to focus on one reason that anti-Semitism has played a role in Christianity: the mistaken notion that God has rejected the Jewish people. Consequently, I have anticipated what I will say next week: God has not rejected the people of Israel.

The homily ends with another Eucharistic conclusion. But in this instance I have noted that when we celebrate the Eucharist we proclaim the death of the *Jewish* Messiah. In this way, I have tried to remind the congregation of Christianity's Jewish roots, which it must never disown.

God's Irrevocable Call
Romans 11:13-15, 29-32

Before the Homily

Today's reading provides homilists with an opportunity to address the question of anti-Semitism by reminding their congregations that God has not rejected the Jewish people: "for the gifts and the call of God are irrevocable" (11:29). But since this text is the conclusion of a long and intricate argument that Paul has been developing since the outset of chapter 9, those who preach from it should read through the whole of Romans 9–11 with a view to the conclusion Paul draws in this reading. Since I have already summarized the argument of these chapters in my synopsis of Romans (see pp. 14–16), I will highlight only three points here.

First, chapter 11 begins with a question that underlies all that Paul writes in these chapters: "has God rejected his people?" (11:1a). The answer that one gives to this question is of utmost importance. If one believes that God has rejected the Jewish people, then there is no place for the Jews in God's economy of salvation. If one thinks that God has rejected the people of Israel, then there is little or no continuity between Israel and the church in God's economy of salvation. In such a view, the church has supplanted Israel as the new people of God.

Paul's resounding "of course not!" (11:1b) should put an end to any notion that God has rejected the Jewish people. Although the greater portion of Paul's contemporaries did not believe in the gospel, Paul was profoundly convinced that God's promises and gifts to Israel (enumerated in last week's reading) have not been revoked. The Jewish people remain God's people.

Second, in chapter 11 Paul specifically addresses the Gentile Christians at Rome in order to remind them that they—a wild olive shoot—have been grafted into the tree of Israel (11:13-24). But just as they have been grafted into the tree of Israel through their faith

75

in the gospel, so those branches of Israel that were cut off can be grafted in again. Thus, Paul hopes for the restoration of Israel.

Third, in the unit that immediately proceeds this one (11:25-28), Paul explains that a temporary hardening has come upon a part of Israel, but when the deliverer (the Messiah) comes forth from Zion "all Israel will be saved" (11:26). This is a rather enigmatic passage, but its sense is this: in God's time, in God's way, God will save Israel through the Messiah.

In the homily that follows I have tried to remind the congregation of the intimate relationship between Judaism and Christianity that makes anti-Semitism incompatible with the Christian faith.

The Homily

Introduction/Exposition. For the past several weeks, the second reading for our Sunday liturgy has been taken from St. Paul's letter to the Romans. Paul, the great Apostle to the Gentiles, struggles to understand and explain the meaning of what God has done for us in Christ.

Fully convinced that God has reconciled the world to himself through the death and resurrection of his Son, St. Paul urges us to accept the gift of forgiveness and redemption that God freely and graciously offers in Jesus Christ. Consequently, throughout this letter *St. Paul reminds us* that we are saved by God's grace rather than by anything we have done. *He reminds us* that our salvation is a gracious gift from God to which we must respond with a lively and obedient faith that trusts and relies in the goodness and graciousness of God.

Exposition. Toward the end of this letter, however, St. Paul addresses a problem that causes him great anguish. Filled with distress because the majority of his Jewish contemporaries have not believed in Jesus as the promised Messiah, Paul takes up the difficult question regarding his own people, the people of Israel. *Does their present lack of faith mean* that God has rejected them? *Does their lack of faith mean* that they will be excluded from the salvation that Christ has brought? *Does their refusal to believe in Jesus as the Messiah mean* that they are no longer God's chosen people?

In today's second reading St. Paul provides an answer to these questions when he writes, "the gifts and the call of God are irrevocable." *Confident that God* always remains faithful to his promises, *St. Paul proclaims* that God has not rejected the Jewish people. *Confident that God's* purpose cannot be forever frustrated, *St. Paul assures us* that God has not revoked the promises he made to the Jewish people through Abraham, Isaac, Jacob, and the prophets. *St. Paul reminds us* that the Jewish people remain God's people, the people from whom the Messiah came, the people whom God chose to be his own.

In today's gospel, when a Gentile woman, a non-Jew, comes to Jesus and begs him to save her daughter, Jesus responds that he was sent only to the lost sheep of the house of Israel. Although these words are harsh, they are a salutary reminder of the priority that the Jewish people enjoy in God's plan of salvation. They are the chosen people of God, the people from whom Jesus was born. During the days of his earthly life, Jesus directed his ministry to them. To be sure, the majority of them did not accept him as the Messiah, but St. Paul reminds us that God has not rejected his people. In a way and a time known only to God, St. Paul says, "all Israel will be saved."

Application. Given the sad history of anti-Semitism that has scarred our history, St. Paul's letter to the Romans is *a salutary reminder* that there is an intimate relationship between Christianity and Judaism that we dare not tear asunder. It is *a salutary reminder* that we worship the same God and share the same Scriptures in the Old Testament. It is a salutary reminder that Christians and Jews are part of the same mysterious plan of God.

Conclusion. As we celebrate this Eucharist, we give thanks for the salvation we have received in Christ, the *Jewish* Messiah. And we pray for the people from whom Jesus the Messiah, the Savior of the world, was born.

After the Homily

This particular homily begins with an introduction that summarizes what Paul has been saying in this letter. Accordingly, I have identified the first part of the homily as an "introduction/ exposition." This extended introduction allows me to remind those members of the congregation who have heard my earlier homilies on Romans where we have been and to summarize the essential meaning of Romans for those who have not heard those homilies. In this section I focus on Paul's teaching on justification without using this technical term, which would be confusing to most Catholic congregations. Accordingly, I speak of being "saved" by God's grace rather than "justified" by God's grace.

Having summarized the central message of the letter, I focus on the question of Israel, a central topic in Romans 9–11. Here I remind the congregation of last week's reading in which Paul speaks of his distress that the majority of his contemporaries have not accepted the gospel. This allows me to raise the question of whether or not Israel remains God's chosen people.

At this point, you will note that I prefer to refer to the Jewish people rather than to Israel. Whereas "Israel" has a religious connotation in the biblical writings, in contemporary parlance it has a political connotation when it refers to the modern state of Israel. Therefore, since some in the congregation might confuse Paul's religious use of Israel with contemporary usage, it seems best to talk about the Jewish people rather than Israel.

In this homily I have made use of the gospel text again, even though the Sunday Lectionary does not normally choose the second reading in light of the gospel in the way that it selects the Old Testament reading in light of the gospel. But in this case, since the gospel highlights Jesus' mission to Israel, I have found it helpful to refer to the gospel reading.

The application of this homily seeks to highlight the intimate connection between Christianity and Judaism. Were I to preach the homily again, I would develop this further. I would omit the section that refers to the gospel so that I could devote more space to an extended discussion of the sad history of anti-Semitism that has often infected Christianity.

Once more the conclusion brings the congregation back to the Eucharist. In doing so it purposely identifies Jesus as the "Jewish Messiah," and it invites the congregation to pray for the people from whom this Jewish Messiah came.

God's Mysterious Ways
Romans 11:33-36

Before the Homily

Today's reading from Romans is the third and final Lectionary text from Romans 9–11. Within the context of these chapters, this text expresses Paul's wonder and astonishment as he stands in awe before the mystery of God's saving economy that embraces Gentile and Jew alike.

The text begins with three observations about God: (1) the inexpressible richness of God's wisdom and knowledge, (2) God's inscrutable judgments, (3) God's mysterious ways. It then asks three rhetorical questions. The first question ("who has known the mind of the Lord?") corresponds to the third observation; the second ("who has been his counselor?") corresponds to the second observation; and the third ("who has given him anything?") corresponds to the first observation. The reading concludes with a doxology that praises God as the origin and goal of all things.

Like the ending of Romans 8, the conclusion of Romans 11 makes an important statement about God. But whereas the ending of Romans 8 affirms that nothing can separate the justified from the love God has for them, the ending of Romans 11 points to the mystery of the divine economy that has been revealed in Jesus Christ. To be sure, Paul understands something of that mystery inasmuch as it has been revealed to him through the gospel. In light of the gospel, however, he also comprehends how little humans know of God's ways. Who would have thought that God would bring about salvation through the death and resurrection of his Son? Who would have thought that God's economy of salvation would embrace Gentiles as well as Jews?

This text provides homilists with an opportunity to remind the congregation of the mystery that is God. While something of God is knowable from nature, as Paul affirms in Romans 2, and

79

while Jesus Christ is the full and perfect revelation of God, there will always be something unknowable and incomprehensible about God. It is this sense of the mystery of God that I have tried to communicate in this homily.

The Homily

Introduction. There are times when all of us realize the limits of our knowledge. At such moments we understand that no matter how much we know, no matter how intelligent we are, the mystery of God is too rich, too deep, too mysterious for us to comprehend. Today's second reading, taken from St. Paul's letter to the Romans, provides an example of what I mean.

Exposition. Throughout this great letter, which we have been reading most of the summer, St. Paul has been struggling with the mystery of God, the mystery of God's redemptive work in Jesus Christ. In the first part of this letter he has explained that since all have sinned, God has freely and graciously redeemed everyone through Christ's saving death and resurrection. Accordingly, our salvation is not a matter of something we have done. Nor is it something we can earn. It is the free and gracious gift of a surprisingly generous God.

Later, in this same letter, Paul takes up the difficult question of God's faithfulness to the Jewish people, the people of Israel. As we heard Paul say last week, the gifts and the call of God are irrevocable; in God's own way, in God's own time, God will find a way to save and redeem his chosen people.

At the end of this long discussion about God, Paul is utterly amazed at the wisdom, the grace, and the generosity of God's plan of salvation. And so, realizing how little he understands of the mystery of God, he proclaims, "Oh the depth of the riches and wisdom and knowledge of God! How inscrutable are his judgments and how unsearchable his ways!" Astounded at the richness of God's mercy that has been revealed in Jesus Christ, Paul knows that he stands before the mystery of God. He stands before a mystery no human being can comprehend.

Application. Consider for a moment the difference between the way in which St. Paul approaches God and the ways in which so many people approach God. For some people, there is little that is mysterious and hidden about God's ways. They are quite sure that they know how God acts or—in their view—should act. They are a bit too confident that they can speak for God and on behalf of God. And so when God does not act in the way they expect, they become disappointed and even angry with God. But this is not the God of Jesus Christ that St. Paul proclaims. For Paul, God is, and God will always remain, mysterious. God is forever beyond our understanding. God's ways will always surprise us.

St. Paul had to learn this lesson in his own life. For example, *he was utterly astounded* to discover that the crucified Jesus was the Son of God. *He was utterly astounded* to learn the new and surprising way that God saved the world through the cross. *He was utterly astounded* to learn the depth and the generosity of God's mercy.

Our lives are always richer when we stand in humility and awe before the mystery of God. *Our lives are always richer* when we understand that God is beyond our understanding. *Our lives are always richer* when we can say with St. Paul, "Oh, the depth of the riches and wisdom and knowledge of God!"

Conclusion. As we celebrate this Eucharist, we ask for the grace to stand in humility before the mystery that is God.

After the Homily

The introduction to this homily announces the theme of the homily: that the mystery of God is beyond human comprehension. However, were I to revise this homily, I would be more specific about the moments when we get a glimpse of our inadequacy before the mystery of God. For example, it is at moments of birth and death, or at times of unexpected grace and judgment that we suddenly understand how little we know about God's mysterious ways.

In the exposition of this homily, I again summarize the central theme of the letter. However, whereas last week I focused on the gracious way in which God saved us, this week I emphasize the mystery of God. I do this because I want to remind the congregation that this letter about our salvation is ultimately a letter about God who graciously saves us through the death and resurrection of his Son.

After summarizing the letter's central point, I remind the congregation of the readings for the past few weeks in which Paul has been dealing with the question of Israel and proclaims that the gifts and the call of God are irrevocable. This brings me to today's reading in which the Apostle looks back with wonder and awe at God's salvific plan.

Having described Paul's sense of wonder and awe before God, in the application I contrast the pedestrian ways in which some people approach the mystery of God. In such an approach, there is no sense of mystery because God has been reduced to human proportion. God acts—should act—as human beings act. When this human God does not meet our expectations, we are disappointed. There is no sense of mystery and awe before such a human god, before such an idol.

In the final paragraphs, I return to the example of Paul who stood in astonishment and wonder when God was revealed in the crucified Jesus. In light of this, I invite the congregation to imitate the example of Paul by standing in awe before the mystery of God. The homily concludes with an invitation to celebrate the Eucharist and to ask for the grace to stand humbly before the divine mystery.

The Moral Life as an Act of Worship
Romans 12:1-2

Before the Homily

The Lectionary draws its final three readings from Romans from the fifth part of the letter, which I have titled "God's Righteousness and the Moral Life of the Justified" (12:1–15:13). This extended moral exhortation consists of two sections. In the first, from which today's reading is taken, Paul describes the shape of love and obedience in the new age (12:1–13:14). Here, his focus is on the need for believers to find their place in the Body of Christ and live in a way that manifests sincere and genuine love. In the second section Paul deals with a conflict between two factions that are endangering the communal life of the Roman Christians.

Although it consists of only two verses, today's reading sets the tone for the moral exhortation that follows. Since each of these verses makes an important statement about Paul's understanding of the morally good life, it will be helpful to say a few words about each.

In the first verse Paul exhorts the Romans to offer their bodies (by which he means their very selves) as a living sacrifice to God. He calls this sacrifice of themselves their "spiritual worship." In saying this, Paul identifies the morally good life as an act of worship. Previous to their incorporation into Christ, every part of their body was a servant of sin (3:13-18; 6:15-23). But now that they have died to sin through their baptism into Christ's death, they can offer their bodies (themselves) to God as a living sacrifice that will be holy and pleasing to God.

In the second verse Paul exhorts the community not to conform itself to the present age but to be transformed by the renewal of their minds that has occurred in Christ. Once more, the Apostle establishes a contrast between the former and present situation of those who are in Christ. When they were in Adam, they could not discern God's will because of the power of sin that ruled over their lives. Now that they are in Christ, their minds have been renewed by the power of the Spirit that empowers them to know and do God's will. Given this new situation, there is no need to be conformed to the old age.

These two verses present the morally good life as the way in which those who are in Christ worship God. The justified no longer conform themselves to the old age. With their minds renewed, they discern and do God's will, which allows them to offer themselves as living sacrifices to God. In the homily that follows I have tried to present the congregation with a new way of thinking about the moral life. Instead of viewing it as a series of obligations, believers should view the moral life as their spiritual worship, their living sacrifice to God.

The Homily

Introduction. Every week, when we gather to celebrate this Eucharist, we offer a perfect sacrifice to God. We assemble in the name of Christ, and we participate in the sacrifice that he offered on the cross. But in today's second reading, which is taken from St. Paul's letter to the Romans, that great Apostle reminds us of another way that we can offer a sacrifice to God every day of our lives. Reminding us of the mercy that God has extended to us, Paul writes, "offer your bodies as a living sacrifice, holy and pleasing to God, your spiritual worship."

Exposition. To understand what Paul means, it is helpful to recall the world in which he lived. In that world, people regularly offered animal sacrifices to God. These sacrifices occurred every day in the temple of Jerusalem, and Paul would have participated in them. But in today's reading, he makes an astounding statement, especially when we remember the world in which he lived. Offer your body, that is, offer your very self, as a living sacrifice that is holy and pleasing to God.

But what does Paul mean? What kind of sacrifice does he have in mind? Paul answers this question when he writes, "do not conform yourselves to this age but be transformed by the renewal of your mind." The sacrifice that Paul has in view, then, is our new way of life. *By conforming ourselves to Christ rather than to this age,* we are offering a pleasing sacrifice to God. *By conforming ourselves to Christ rather than to this age*, we live a life that is pleasing and holy to God. *By conforming ourselves to Christ, rather than to this age*, we are offering God what Paul calls our "spiritual worship."

Application. For some believers the Christian life is a matter of dos and don'ts: things they must avoid and things they ought to do. When people approach the Christian life in this way, the morally good life becomes a burden. Such a view of the Christian life reduces life in Christ to a series of rules and commandments: laws that must be observed under the penalty of sin and the threat of punishment. But this is not how Paul understood the morally good life; nor is it the way that we should understand it today.

For St. Paul, the morally good life is a grateful response to something God has done for us. *For St. Paul, the morally good life* is a grateful response to the mercy that God has extended to us in Christ. *For St. Paul, the morally good life* is something made possible by the presence of Christ and the Spirit in our lives. *For St. Paul, the morally good life* is an act of worship. The morally good life is our daily sacrifice of praise to God.

Consider how different our lives would be if we approached the Christian moral life in this way. *We would no longer* think of the moral life in terms of rules and regulations. *We would no longer* think of the moral life as a burden or obligation. *We would begin to understand that a morally good life* is the outcome of all that God has done for us. *We would begin to understand that the morally good life* is the expression of gratitude for the gift of salvation we have received. The morally good life would be our act of worship, a pleasing sacrifice that we offer God every day.

Conclusion. At the beginning of this homily I noted that every time we gather to celebrate the Eucharist, we offer a perfect sacrifice of praise to God; and this is true. *Nothing* can surpass the sacrifice that Christ offered the Father. *Nothing* is more pleasing to God than the perfect obedience of the Son. By joining the daily sacrifice of our lives to the perfect sacrifice of Christ, we enter into the mystery of Christ. By offering ourselves to God through the morally good life, we participate more fully in the perfect sacrifice of Christ. As we continue our celebration of this Eucharist, we ask for the grace to be transformed, rather than conformed to this age, so that we worship God by our lives. In this way we will offer God a sacrifice that is living, holy, and pleasing.

After the Homily

I introduce this homily by reminding the congregation that the Eucharist we celebrate is our participation in Christ's perfect sacrifice. By doing this I am preparing the congregation for my central theme: the morally good life is a living sacrifice to God; it is our spiritual worship. In the conclusion I return to the theme of the Eucharist as sacrifice to show the relationship between Christ's sacrifice in which we participate and the living sacrifice of our lives.

In the exposition my goal is to explain what Paul means by a living sacrifice and how we can offer such a sacrifice to God. To accomplish this it is necessary to say something about sacrifice in the ancient world, which was a rather bloody and messy affair, although it is not necessary to develop this aspect of sacrifice in the homily. The point I want to communicate is this: whereas in the ancient world sacrifice consisted in pouring out the blood of the animal, Paul has in view a living sacrifice that is offered through the morally good life.

The questions in the second paragraph of the exposition—"But what does Paul mean?" "What kind of sacrifice does he have in mind?"—begin the process of relating the notion of sacrifice to the ethical life of the believer. Since those who are listening to this text for the first time will not be aware that this is the beginning of Paul's moral exhortation, it is unlikely that they will relate what he is saying about sacrifice to the morally good. Therefore, it is necessary to make this explicit for the congregation. I have tried to do this by highlighting Paul's exhortation that we should not conform ourselves to this age.

The application begins with the way in which some Christians view the moral life: they focus on legal obligations and forget the gracious aspect of life in Christ. My purpose is not to do away with the law but to show that a legalistic view of the Christian life does not cohere with what Paul writes in this letter. Accordingly, the second paragraph of the exposition makes extensive use of repetition to emphasize that this is not how St. Paul understood the moral life of the justified.

Having established a contrast between two views of the moral life—one grounded in law and the other in grace—in the final part of the application I invite the congregation to imagine how different their lives would be if they approached the Christian life as an act of worship rather than as a series of moral obligations.

The homily ends with a longer than usual conclusion in which I relate the sacrifice we offer when we gather for the Eucharist to the sacrifice we offer God through a morally good life. Here it is important for me to show the congregation that these two acts of worship are complementary rather than opposed to each other. By offering themselves as a living sacrifice to God through the morally good lives they live, the justified participate ever more profoundly in the perfect sacrifice of the Eucharist.

Love, the Fulfillment of the Law
Romans 13:8-10

Before the Homily

Today's reading is the conclusion to the first part of the moral exhortation that began in last week's reading. Consequently, homilists should read through the whole exhortation (12:1–13:14) before proceeding to this text. As they do, they should note two things. First, in Rom 12:9-21 Paul provides the Romans with an extended description of what he means by genuine love. This instruction will help homilists understand what Paul intends by love in this text. Second, today's reading follows a unit in which Paul encourages the Romans to be subordinate to those in authority by paying taxes to those to whom they are due. The manner in which today's reading begins ("Owe nothing to anyone . . ."), then, is a play on the words "due" and "owe." Although believers must pay taxes to those to whom they are *due*, their deepest and most important debt is the debt of love that they *owe* to their neighbor.

This reading is important for understanding Romans since it responds to a perennial problem: If we are saved/justified on the basis of God's grace through trusting faith in Jesus Christ, doesn't this teaching open the door to antinomianism? Doesn't it imply that there is no room in Paul's theology for the law? Doesn't it suggest that it doesn't matter what we do so long as we believe? For a trenchant critique of this mistaken view of Paul's teaching, see the letter of James (2:14-26).

In today's reading Paul explains that the justified fulfill the law through the love commandment of Lev 19:18 ("You shall love your neighbor as yourself"). Quoting four commandments from the Decalogue as examples of the law, he says that these and any other commandments are summed up in the love commandment. Since the love commandment requires one to do what is for the neighbor's good, it is the fulfillment of the law.

Paul's teaching on justification does not dismiss the law as if it were no longer relevant. In Romans 7 Paul affirms that the law is holy and that the commandment of God is righteous and good (7:12). The issue for Paul, then, is not the goodness of the law and its commandments but how the law is to be fulfilled. In light of the gospel, he affirms that the deepest meaning of the law is summed up and fulfilled in the love command, for love does no harm to the neighbor.

In the homily that follows I have raised the problem occasioned by Paul's teaching on justification and how Paul resolves this issue through his understanding of the central role that the love commandment plays in the Christian life.

The Homily

Introduction. Since the beginning of this summer, we have been listening to parts of St. Paul's most important letter, his great letter to the Romans. In this letter the Apostle has been speaking about the faithfulness of God and the unexpected way in which God saves us. Again and again Paul has said that we have been saved by God's grace. We have been saved by Christ's death and resurrection. In other words, our salvation is not the result of something we have done but what God has done for us in Christ. From start to finish, from beginning to end, our salvation is a gracious gift from a gracious God who has graciously shown his love for us in Christ.

Exposition/Application. But now, as St. Paul comes to the end of this letter, he turns his attention to the Christian life. *If salvation is God's gracious gift to us,* how are we to act? *If salvation is something that God has done for us,* how are we to respond? How are we to respond to God who has been so gracious and loving to us?

We heard part of the answer to this question last week when St. Paul encouraged us to offer ourselves to God as a living sacrifice, holy and pleasing to God. Paul calls this our spiritual worship. Paul told us that our lives are an act of worship when we live in accordance with God's will. For when we live our Christian life according to the gospel, we are worshiping and praising the God who has saved us.

Today St. Paul gives us another answer to the question of how we should live our Christian lives. What are we to do? How should we respond to God's love for us? Paul's answer is quite simple: owe nothing to anyone except to love one another, for love is the fulfillment of God's law. Paul goes on to list the command-ments and concludes that love is the fulfillment of the law because it does no harm to our neighbor. So the short answer to the ques-tion—how should we live the Christian life?—is that we should love one another.

But what is Paul's understanding of love? What does he mean when he says that love is the fulfillment of the law? To answer this question we need to recall God's love for us—the love that Christ manifested on the cross. For St. Paul, Christ's death on the cross is the perfect expression of love, the perfect expression of the total gift of giving oneself for others. *Christ did not die* for himself but for us. *Christ did not die* to atone for his sins but for our sins. The death of Christ, then, is the perfect expression of love.

In today's second reading, St. Paul writes that all the com-mandments are fulfilled in one commandment: "You shall love your neighbor as yourself." He then goes on to say that love does no evil toward the neighbor. Here, then, is the perfect expression of the Christian life. *If we want to live* the Christian life in a way that is holy and pleasing to God, we will live as Christ did: we will love our neighbor as Christ loved us. *If we want our life* to be an act of worship, we will worship God by imitating the unselfish love of Christ.

Conclusion. As we celebrate this Eucharist, the perfect expres-sion of Christ's love for us, we ask for the grace to love each other, to love our neighbor, as Christ loved us.

After the Homily

In the introduction to this homily I remind the congregation that we have been listening to readings from Romans for most of the summer. I then summarize the main theme of the letter (that we have been saved by God's grace rather than by what we have done). In doing this, I am setting up the question I will address in the body of the homily. As has been my practice throughout these homilies, I employ the vocabulary of save/salvation rather than justify/justification, since the former word group is more familiar to most Roman Catholics than the latter.

The body of this particular homily does not have neatly defined sections of exposition and application. What follows is primarily an exposition of how Paul understands the moral life in light of his teaching on justification. In this particular case, however, I think it is fair to say that the exposition of Paul's teaching borders on application, since this particular exposition illustrates how love fulfills the prescriptions of God's law.

This exposition begins with a question that identifies the central theme of the homily: if salvation is God's gift to us, how should we live our lives? In response to this question, I provide two answers. First, I recall last week's reading in which Paul described the morally good life of the justified as the way in which they offer themselves to God. Second, I turn to today's reading in which Paul affirms that love is the fulfillment of the law.

Although most Christians might readily agree that love is at the heart of the Christian moral life, it is important to understand what Paul means by love, since contemporary culture tends to reduce love to an emotion or feeling. Accordingly, I provide two answers to this question. The first is based on the kind of love that God manifested for humanity through Jesus' death on the cross for the godless. The second answer returns to the reading for the day in which Paul describes love as doing what is good for the neighbor. Christian love, then, is more than a feeling or emotion: it is a matter of doing what is good toward others, even when there is little or no feeling or emotion in our love for the other.

The homily ends with another brief conclusion that reminds the congregation of the Eucharist they are about to receive. Here, I encourage the congregation to pray for the grace to love each other as Christ loved us. In saying this, I am suggesting that just as our justification/salvation is a gift, so our ability to respond to the gift is a gift for which we must pray.

The Lord of the Living and of the Dead
Romans 14:7-9

Before the Homily

The Lectionary concludes its reading of Romans with a text that occurs in the second section of Paul's moral exhortation, which I have titled "Receiving Each Other according to the Example of Christ" (14:1–15:13). In this section of his moral exhortation Paul is addressing tensions that have arisen between two factions within the Roman community. One faction, which Paul identifies as those who are weak in faith, continues to observe Jewish dietary prescriptions and certain days as more important than others. The other faction, which he calls the strong, does not. Although Paul belongs to the strong, since his faith in Christ convinces him that he is no longer bound by such ritual prescriptions (15:1), he does not take up the cause of the strong. Instead, aware that the weak are acting according to their faith in Christ, he encourages the strong to welcome "anyone who is weak in faith" (14:1). Moreover, he insists: "We who are strong ought to put up with the failings of the weak and not to please ourselves" (15:1).

Paul's purpose in Rom 14:1–15:13 is to bring these two factions together. Each faction should welcome the other in the way that Christ welcomed them (15:7). This inclusive ethic seeks to overcome the differences among the Roman Christians by reminding them that the gospel they have embraced is more important than the social differences that divide them. Today, we would say that faith in Christ is more important than the cultural issues that divide us.

Today's reading, which is only a small selection from this moral exhortation, provides the Romans with a powerful reason why their faith in Christ is more important than the differences that threaten to tear apart the fabric of their life in Christ. He argues that the purpose of their new life in Christ is not to live for themselves but for the one who is "Lord of both the dead and the living" (14:9).

This text provides homilists with an opportunity to remind their congregations that faith in Christ is more embracing and inclusive than the petty differences that threaten to divide the Body of Christ. Before preaching from this text homilists should read through the whole of Paul's argument in Rom 14:1–15:13. Although they need not explain the entire section to the congregation, they must to be aware of what it says if they hope to interpret the text for their congregation.

The Homily

Introduction. Nothing is more destructive to the Christian life than factions and divisions within the Christian community, whether it be in the universal church or the local parish community. *When the church is divided,* Christians no longer give a unified witness to Christ. *When the parish community is divided,* parishioners no longer treat each other as members of the Body of Christ. *At such moments,* our differences become more important than the gospel we proclaim. *At such moments,* our opinions become more important than the faith in Christ that we profess. *At such moments,* we no longer welcome each other as Christ welcomed us.

Exposition. Although we often think of the period of the early church as an idyllic time when there were no divisions within the church—a period when everyone believed in the Lord in the same way—it was not so. *We know* from St. Paul's letters to the Corinthians that there were factions in the church at Corinth. *We know* from his letter to the Romans that there were tensions and divisions among the Roman Christians as well. Whereas some were convinced that their faith in Christ no longer required them to follow certain prescriptions of the Jewish law that once bound them, others were not so sure, and so they continued to observe these laws.

Aware of the factions and divisions that threatened to separate believer from believer, Paul concludes his letter to the Romans with a call to unity. He reminds both factions that they now live for the Lord who died for them. Consequently, whether they live or whether they die, they belong to the Lord.

Application. These are difficult days for society and church. If you listen to talk radio or cable news, you know that we are in the midst of a destructive culture war that threatens to divide the church as well as our country. For example, people listen to the commentators with whom they agree. They only read those newspapers and journals that reinforce what they already believe. They prefer to associate with those who share their opinions rather than with those who think differently.

To be sure, this behavior is natural. It is always easier to be with people with whom we agree. *But when we begin to think* that there is only one way to think, we become intolerant of others. *When we begin to think* that we are the only ones who know the truth, we no longer trust each other.

Do not misunderstand. I am not saying that we should sacrifice the truth by accepting every opinion. Nor am I advocating that every view is right. Rather, I am suggesting that *there are moments when we need* to understand the other point of view. *There are moments when we need* to be more attentive to what others are saying.

This should come as no surprise to us who believe in Christ as the Lord of the living and the dead. *For us,* faith in Christ is more important than the petty things that separate us. *For us,* the gospel of Christ is more important than the political ideology of the day. *For us,* the unity of the Body of Christ is more important than the cultural and ethnic divisions that surround us and threaten to divide us.

Notice what Paul says to the Romans: Christ died and rose so that "he might be the Lord of both the dead and the living." Christ died so that we might belong to him. Christ died so that we might live for him. He did not die so that we might live for ourselves; he died so that we might live for him.

Conclusion. *In celebrating this Eucharist,* we publicly confess that we belong to the one who is the Lord of the living and the dead. *In sharing this Eucharist,* we confess that we belong to the Body of Christ. *By gathering for this Eucharist* week after week, we acknowledge that what unites us in Christ is more important than what divides us. We proclaim that our faith in Christ is more important than what separates us. As we eat the body and drink from the cup, then, we ask for the grace to live as one in Christ, the Lord of the living and of the dead.

After the Homily

The introduction to this homily establishes the theme for what follows: the danger that factions and divisions pose for the life of the church. I have made extensive use of repetition in this introduction to highlight why divisions and factions are so dangerous for the believing community: at such moments, people make their personal convictions more important than the gospel they claim to espouse.

In the exposition I make two points. First, there never was an idyllic period in the early church when there were no divisions and tensions within the Christian community. The difficulties with which Paul had to deal at Corinth testify to this. Second, I summarize the situation among the Christians at Rome to explain what I mean. Here, some homilists may want to give more background than I have, but it seems to me that a few words of explanation are all that is needed.

In the application of this particular homily I begin with a reference to the cultural wars that currently divide American society. Although this reference will resonate with most people in the pew, it also presents a problem, since many parishes are deeply divided by these cultural wars. Lest homilists be viewed as partisans for one side or the other, they must find a way to stand above the fray. In doing so they will provide their congregations with an example of how to do the same. I have reminded members of the congregation that our common faith in Christ and the gospel is more important than the cultural and social issues that threaten to divide us.

In addition to reminding the congregation of the unity we have in the gospel, I have highlighted the need for tolerance. This also presents a problem, since some view tolerance as relativism. Accordingly, I have assured the congregation that I am not setting aside truth for the sake of tolerance. Rather, my purpose is to encourage those with differing opinions to listen to each other so that they can understand why others think differently, even if they do not agree with them.

The homily has a longer than usual conclusion in which I highlight the significance of what we do each time we assemble to celebrate the Eucharist: we proclaim the unity we enjoy in Christ. It is this unity that is always more important than the differences that divide us.

Preaching from Romans 3 during the Week

In addition to playing an important role in the Sunday Lectionary, Romans has a vital role in the Weekday Lectionary as well. In the weekday readings for Year 1 (2011, 2013, 2015, etc.), there is a semi-continuous reading from Romans from the twenty-eighth through the thirty-first weeks of the year. Since these readings are longer and more complete than the readings of the Sunday cycle, they provide preachers with an opportunity to probe more deeply into this letter so that they can preach Romans with confidence when it occurs in Year A of the Sunday cycle.

Preaching at daily Mass, however, is a different experience from preaching on Sunday. In most instances, the homily will be shorter and less developed, even though the readings are longer and more complex. Moreover, given the length and complexity of some of the readings, there will probably be more need for exposition and explanation of the text, to which the homilist will add a brief application. Those who do preach from Romans during the week have one advantage they do not enjoy on Sunday: the congregation to which they preach will probably consist of the same people day in and day out. Thus preachers find themselves in the enviable position of being able to build upon what they have said in earlier homilies in a way they cannot do when preaching on Sundays. In the context of the daily liturgy, then, homilists become teachers as well as preachers inasmuch as they provide their small group of committed believers with a deeper and more profound understanding of the Scriptures.

Given the nature of the daily homily, I have chosen to present brief expositions of these readings rather than sample homilies, in the hope that these explanations of the text will encourage preachers to present their own homilies on Romans, tailored to the particular needs of their congregation.

Monday: A Summary of the Gospel (Rom 1:1-7)

Unlike the Sunday Lectionary, which passes over most of the first three chapters of Romans, the Weekday Lectionary begins with the opening greeting of the letter. This is the longest and most detailed greeting of any Pauline letter. The reason for this is that Paul was not the founder of the church at Rome, and he had not yet visited the Christians there. Consequently, he begins his letter with an extended greeting in order to introduce himself to the Romans and summarize the gospel he preaches among the Gentiles.

Paul describes himself in two ways: as a slave/servant of Jesus Christ and as an Apostle who has been consecrated or set apart for "the gospel of God," by which Paul means God's own good news of what God has done for humanity in the saving death and resurrection of his Son. In saying that he was set apart for this gospel, Paul reminds the Romans of his apostolic call when God revealed his Son to him (see Gal 1:15-17).

In addition to identifying himself as a slave/servant and Apostle, Paul provides the Romans with a brief summary of the gospel he preaches. The gospel of God that he proclaims is the gospel about God's Son whom Paul describes in two ways. In terms of his human origin, Jesus was a descendant of David; he was the royal messiah. In terms of his divine origin, he is the Son of God who was established as Son of God in power when God raised him from the dead.

Having identified himself and summarized the content of his gospel, Paul explains the purpose of his apostleship: "to bring about the obedience of faith" (1:5). This expression, which could be the theme of the homily, refers to the obedience that faith entails: complete and utter obedience to the gospel of God. Those who listen to Romans for the next four weeks will be challenged to practice this obedience in their own lives.

Tuesday: The Root of All Sin (Rom 1:16-25)

Today's reading announces the theme of Paul's letter: the righteousness of God. Paul is not ashamed of the gospel because it is the power of God that leads to salvation for all who believe in it. Moreover, when the gospel is proclaimed, God's saving righteousness, by which Paul means God's covenant faithfulness and loyalty, is revealed. Paul affirms that this saving righteousness is available to all who believe and entrust themselves to God.

Having announced the revelation of God's saving righteousness in the opening verses of this reading, Paul turns his attention to the wrath of God. While most people think of God's wrath as an emotion, Paul uses the term in another way: the wrath of God is God's just judgment against sin.

In Rom 1:18-32 Paul explains that the wrath/judgment of God is coming upon the Gentile (non-Jewish) world because it failed to acknowledge God. Although it knew something of God from the created world, the Gentile world suppressed the truth about God and exchanged the glory of God for mere images and idols. According to Paul's analysis of the human condition, this idolatry is the root of all sin; it is the sin from which all other sins grow and develop.

Since the Gentiles refused to acknowledge God as God, God handed them over to their own sinfulness. Thus the punishment for sin is sin! Because sinful humanity refuses to acknowledge the truth about God, it must live in a godless world of its own making.

In preaching from this text homilists might focus on the root of all sin: the human refusal to acknowledge God as God. Or, they might deal with the Pauline notion of God's wrath in which the punishment for sin is to live in sin. Those who refuse to acknowledge God's glory are condemned to live in a world of their own making without God.

Wednesday: The Impartiality of God (Rom 2:1-11)

In this well-defined unit, Paul turns his attention to an imaginary listener who foolishly supposes that he or she will be able to escape God's judgment. The imaginary listener that Paul has in view hypocritically approves of Paul's condemnation of the Gentile world that we heard yesterday, even though he or she does the same things. Attacking this hypocrisy of someone who thinks that he or she is superior to others, Paul reminds his listener of the impending judgment of God that will be based on what a person has done or failed to do. Those who have persevered in doing good will be given eternal life, whereas those who have disobeyed the truth and chosen the way of wickedness will experience God's wrath on the day of judgment.

The main point that Paul makes comes at the end of this reading: "There is no partiality with God" (2:11). God does not judge people on the basis of who they are but on the basis of what they do or fail to do. For those who think that Paul's doctrine of justification does away with the moral life, this text is a salutary reminder that the justified and reconciled must continue to do good.

A homily on this passage could focus on the danger of judging others, since those who judge others inevitably do what they condemn others for doing. Or, the homily might develop the theme of the impartiality of God, who does not judge people on the basis of who they are but on the basis of what they do or fail to do.

Thursday: No Boasting before God (Rom 3:21-30)

At this point, the Lectionary skips over a great deal of material with which homilists should familiarize themselves before considering this reading: Paul's indictment of Jewish failure to observe the law (2:17-29) and Paul's final conclusion that Gentiles and Jews are under the power of sin (3:1-20). Pay special attention to Rom 3:9, however, in which Paul states that all, without exception, are under the enslaving power of sin.

Paul's indictment that *all*, Jew as well as Gentile, are under the power of sin (3:9) brings us to today's reading. Since all are under the power of sin, all are in need of salvation. Returning to the theme of God's righteousness introduced in Tuesday's reading, Paul explains that since all have sinned and fallen short of God's glory, God has rescued all people by revealing his saving righteousness in the death of Christ.

Paul describes the effects of this saving righteousness in several ways: (1) believers have been freely justified/acquitted by God; (2) believers have been redeemed or bought back from their slavery to sin. Consequently, their sins have be expiated, atoned for, and forgiven by the blood of Christ.

Because of God's saving righteousness in Christ, there is no room for human beings to boast of their accomplishments before God. Human beings have not, and cannot, justify or redeem themselves. They cannot declare themselves innocent before God. Nor can they restore the relationship with God that they have broken. Rather, they have been justified and redeemed by God, who made Christ a means of atonement for their sins. The Pauline teaching of justification by faith, then, means that we are put in a right relationship with God on the basis of what God has done for us rather than on the basis of what we have done for God.

Given the density and complexity of this passage, homilists will do well to focus on a single point, such as the gracious nature of salvation or the folly of thinking that God is indebted to us. From start to finish everything is a matter of God's grace and favor. This is why there is no room for human boasting before God.

Friday: Abraham Believed (Rom 4:1-8)

Since the readings for the next three days will be taken from Romans 4, this is a good time to become acquainted with this chapter. Preachers ought to read through the whole chapter several times. As they do so, they should keep in mind that Paul is explaining the text of Gen 15:6 as quoted in Rom 4:3: "Abraham believed God, and it was credited to him as righteousness."

The text for today's reading is the opening unit of this chapter. Its intent is to present Abraham as a model of faith: someone whom God justified because he trusted in God's promise. At the end of chapter 3, Paul asked if his teaching on justification annuls the law (3:31). In response to that question, he turns to the example of Abraham, to whom God credited righteousness (a status of being in a right relation with God) because he believed in God's promise.

The argument that Paul presents in this text is complex, and most congregations will be puzzled by it. But the main point that Paul makes is clear: Abraham is an example of someone who was justified before God on the basis of his trusting faith in God's promise rather than on the basis of anything he did.

Homilists should review the story of God's promise to Abraham as narrated in Genesis 15, since Paul's argument presupposes knowledge of this account. If they are familiar with this story, they will be able to develop a homily on this text that highlights Abraham's trusting faith in God's promise.

Saturday: Abraham Trusted the Promise (Rom 4:13, 16-18)

In this passage Paul explains that the promise God made to Abraham depends on faith rather than on the law. If the promise depended on the law, the promise would only be accessible to the adherents of the law. But if God's promise depends on faith, as Paul affirms, then the promise is available to all, to Gentiles as well as to Jews, who exhibit the same trusting faith that Abraham did.

In this text, and throughout this letter, Paul is seeking a way to bring Gentiles and Jews together. This is why the way of faith is so important for him. For whereas the law excludes those who are not circumcised, the way of faith embraces the uncircumcised as well as the circumcised.

Abraham, then, is a unifying figure for Paul. He is the physical ancestor of the Jewish people and the spiritual ancestor of Gentiles who believe with the same kind of faith that he exhibited.

Toward the end of today's reading Paul describes this faith as faith in the God "who gives life to the dead." A homily on this passage might focus on the nature of Abraham's faith that, for Paul, has become a model of Christian faith. Christians do not merely believe in God; they believe in God who raises the dead.

Monday: These Things Were Written for Our Sake (Rom 4:20-25)

In Romans 4 Paul has been delivering something akin to a homily in which he has been explaining the meaning of Gen 15:6: "Abraham believed God, and it was credited to him as righteousness" (as quoted in Rom 4:3). In today's reading the Apostle brings his homily to a close and applies it to his congregation.

First, Paul explains that Abraham's faith was credited to him as righteousness because he did not doubt God's promise. Instead, he was confident that God was able to do what he promised, even though there was no human reason to believe in the promise. In other words, Abraham's faith was an act of utter trust in the power of God rather than in the human possibility that God's promise of offspring could or would be fulfilled. This is why God credited or counted Abraham's faith/trust as righteousness.

Next, before concluding his homily on Gen 15:6, Paul does what all good homilists do. He applies the scriptural text he has been explaining to the lives of his congregation. Fully convinced that Scripture is a living Word that speaks to every generation, Paul affirms that the text of Genesis applies to us as well as to Abraham when we believe in God who raised Jesus from the dead. In this way the Apostle draws a close relationship between the faith of Abraham and the faith of Christians. Just as Abraham trusted in the power of God to fulfill the promise of offspring, even though Abraham was advanced in age and Sarah's womb was as good as dead, so Christians trust in the power of God who raised the dead Christ from the tomb.

The final words of today's reading read like a creedal formula inasmuch as they describe the effects of Jesus' death and resurrection: Jesus handed himself over for our sins, and God raised him from the dead in order to justify us.

This text provides homilists with an opportunity to draw a comparison between the faith of Abraham and the faith of those who believe in Christ. In both instances, faith trusts in the power of God to do what, from a purely human perspective, is impossible. Such faith trusts in God who brings life out of death.

Tuesday: There Is No Comparison
(Rom 5:12, 15b, 17-19, 20b-21)

The Lectionary moves from the example of Abraham to the comparison of Adam and Christ. In doing so it passes over Rom 5:1-11, a passage in which Paul describes the new situation of believers who are at peace with God because God has justified and reconciled them to himself through the death and resurrection of his Son. Justified and reconciled to God, believers can be all the more confident that they will be saved from death at the general resurrection of the dead.

In 5:12-21 Paul explains that this came about through the obedience of Christ, the new Adam, who counteracted the disobedience of the old Adam. Thus the text draws a comparison between the disobedience of the man who introduced sin and death into the world and the obedience of the man who brought life and grace into the world. But as I have already noted, when commenting on the use of this text for the Eleventh Week of Ordinary Time in Year A, this is a difficult and confusing text.

First, at the outset of this reading Paul begins a comparison he does not conclude (5:12). Next, before concluding his comparison, he makes a number of qualifications to show that there really is no comparison between Adam and Christ (5:15b, 17). Finally, Paul completes the comparison he began but did not finish (5:18-19), and he concludes that where sin increased, God's grace abounded all the more (5:20b-21).

I make two points here. First, there really is no comparison between Adam and Christ, for whereas the transgression of Adam brought the rule of death, the gift of justification came with Jesus Christ. Second, when we compare Adam and Christ, we see that whereas the disobedience of Adam resulted in many becoming sinners, the obedience of Christ resulted in many being made righteous.

Although it will always be a challenge to preach this text, preachers should not shy away from the task since its central point is of immense importance to the Christian life. We do not belong to Adam, the father of the old humanity, but to Christ, who has inaugurated a new humanity characterized by grace and righteousness. To be in Christ is to be justified. To be under grace is to live in the realm of God's life.

Wednesday: Do Not Let Sin Rule Over You (Rom 6:12-18)

At this point the Lectionary passes over Rom 6:1-11, in which Paul argues that believers are no longer under the power of sin, since they died to sin when they associated themselves with Christ's death by baptism into Christ. Therefore, since believers are no longer under of the power of sin, they should not continue to sin.

In today's reading Paul continues this theme from a slightly different vantage point. First, he exhorts the Romans not to allow sin to rule over them. Their bodies should no longer be "weapons" that sin uses for the sake of wickedness. Instead of putting their bodies (themselves) at the service of sin, they must use their bodies (themselves) as "weapons" in the service of righteousness, for they are no longer under the regime of the law but of God's grace. This last remark, which Paul makes in Rom 5:14, leads to an objection to his gospel. If we are no longer under the law, doesn't this mean that we can do anything we want?

Paul is not advocating an antinomian way of life, as the rest of today's reading shows. His point is this: we are always slaves or servants to something or someone, since we always give our allegiance to someone or something. When we were "in Adam," we were slaves of sin. But now that we are "in Christ," we have becomes slaves of righteousness. We are no longer under the law, by which Paul means that we no longer belong to the old age as defined by Adam. Now that we are "in Christ," we belong to the realm of grace in which we serve God in righteousness.

A homily on this text might begin with the observation that human beings always give themselves to someone or something. True wisdom is giving oneself to the right person and the right cause. For Christians, the right person is Jesus Christ and the right cause is the gospel. People who understand this will comprehend why sin is no longer an option for those who believe in Christ.

Thursday: The Wage of Sin and the Gift of God (Rom 6:19-23)

Today's reading is a continuation of yesterday's text. At the end of that reading Paul reminded the Romans that having been set free from sin, they have become slaves of righteousness (6:18).

With this statement he reinforces the basic thesis that he is propounding in this section: we are always slaves or servants to someone or something. Consequently, freedom from sin does not lead to license but to service to another master whose gift is eternal life.

Paul begins somewhat apologetically. He knows that the metaphor he is employing is offensive to some of the Romans, since many of them were slaves. But this is precisely why he uses it. Living in a society where slavery was the economic engine of the day, the Roman Christians understood what slavery involved: complete and total obedience to one's master.

Building on this metaphor, Paul reminds the Romans that when they were slaves of sin, the wage they received was death. The death that Paul has in view is more than physical death; it is eternal and irreversible separation from God. But now that they have been set free from sin and become God's slaves, they have received the gift of eternal life. Notice that Paul does not say that they have received the *wage* of eternal life, since that would imply that believers can earn their salvation. Rather, he emphasizes that "slavery" to God results in a gift that one could never earn: unending life with God.

A homily on this text might remind the congregation that the decision to give our allegiance to someone or something has profound consequences. If we align ourselves with the old Adam, our wage will be eternal separation from God. If we align ourselves with Christ, the new Adam, God will graciously give us the gift of his own life.

Friday: The Conflicted Self (Rom 7:18-25a)

At different points in Romans, Paul has described what the human condition apart from God's grace is like. In today's reading he presents a classic description of the conflicted self: a person who knows God's will but cannot do God's will because he or she is overpowered by the power of sin.

What Paul writes here is not a purely autobiographical statement, nor is it a description of humankind in general. Rather, it is a portrayal of the human condition *viewed and understood in light of the gospel*. In light of the gospel, Paul looks at the human situation and judges that apart from the grace of God we may know God's will, but we cannot do God's will because the power of sin always overwhelms us.

The person that Paul describes here is the unredeemed person who knows something of God and even wants to do God's will but cannot. This is the situation of humankind in the old Adam. It is the situation of every person apart from God's grace.

At the end of this reading, this unredeemed person cries out and asks who will rescue him from his mortal body that is destined for death. Paul's response, which is a prelude to chapter 8, is Jesus Christ. It is Jesus Christ who redeems unredeemed humanity from its bondage to sin and death. It is Jesus Christ who provides an alternative to the old Adam.

This is a text that will resonate with the congregation, since most people experience conflict within themselves at one time or another. They want to do what is good, but they do not. When preaching this text, however, it is important to remember that Paul is speaking of unredeemed humanity rather than redeemed humanity. Consequently, the homily should emphasize that those who are in Christ find themselves in a new situation that God has made possible in Christ: they know and they can do God's will.

Saturday: In the Spirit Rather than in the Flesh (Rom 8:1-11)

With this reading the Weekday Lectionary begins the first of five readings on Romans 8, which is Paul's most important statement about the role of the Spirit in the Christian life.

The beginning of this chapter (8:1-4) provides a further answer to the desperate cry that we heard from the conflicted self in yesterday's reading. Those who are in Christ are no longer liable to condemnation. The Spirit has done what the Mosaic Law could not do; it has freed them from the cosmic powers of sin and death. God accomplished this by sending his own Son in "the likeness of sinful flesh" (8:3). This means that the Son took on the fullness of the human condition by entering into the sphere of sin (without sinning). There the Son overcame the power of sin on its own battlefield, the battlefield of the flesh.

Having explained how God rescued humanity from the power of sin through his own Son and the power of the Spirit, in the remainder of this reading Paul draws a sharp contrast between the realm of the flesh (all that is mortal and destined to die) and the realm of God's Spirit (all that is immortal and cannot die). Formerly, when they were in the old Adam, the Romans were in the realm of the flesh. Now that they are in Christ, they are in the realm of the Spirit. When they were in the realm of the flesh, they could not please God; now that they are in the realm of the Spirit they can. Furthermore, since the Spirit dwells in them, they can be confident that just as God raised Jesus from the dead, so God will raise them from the dead. The Spirit, then, is their assurance of resurrection life.

There are few texts more important for the Christian life than this text, which describes the Christian life as life in the Spirit. A homily on this text will try to clarify for the congregation the difference between living according to the flesh and living according to the Spirit. It will remind the congregation that to live according to the flesh is to set one's hope on all that is mortal and perishable, whereas to live according to the Spirit is to set one's hope on all that is immortal and imperishable.

Monday: Free from the Flesh, Children of God
(Rom 8:12-17)

Today's reading is a continuation of Saturday's text in which Paul describes the new life believers enjoy in the Spirit. In that lesson Paul reminded the Romans that they are no longer in the realm of the flesh but in the realm of God's Spirit (8:9) because of what God has done for them in Christ. Today's reading builds upon that reading in two ways.

First, Paul draws an important conclusion from what he has been saying (8:12-13). Those who are in Christ are no longer "debtors to the flesh" (8:12). That is, they are not obligated to do the selfish deeds that characterize living according to the flesh. Should they persist in that old way of life that characterizes life "in Adam," they will surely die. Here, Paul has in view something more than physical death. Those who conduct their lives according to the old standards of the flesh will be eternally separated from God, who is the source of life. They will forfeit the newness of life they already enjoy in Christ. But if they put to death their old way of life and live according to the Spirit, they will live. That is, they will enjoy the newness of life that comes from the Spirit.

Second, Paul reminds the Romans of their true situation by speaking of their new relation with God and the inheritance they are about to receive. Inasmuch as they are led by God's Spirit, they have become God's sons and daughters in a way that reflects Christ's sonship. The Spirit they have received allows them to call God *Abba* ("Father"), the way in which Jesus himself addressed God. As God's adopted sons and daughters, then, they enjoy a new relationship with God patterned on Jesus' relationship to God.

But there is more. If they are God's adopted children, they are related to Christ in a new way: they have become "joint heirs with Christ" (8:17). That is, they will receive the same inheritance into which Jesus, the Son of God, has already entered, namely, resurrection life. But to enter into this inheritance and be glorified with Christ, they must suffer with Christ. They must make the pattern of Christ's life the pattern of their lives.

A homily on this text could focus on one of three points: (1) the need to live in accordance with God's Spirit rather than according to the urging of the flesh, (2) the new status that believers enjoy as God's adopted sons and daughters, (3) the inheritance of resurrection life they will receive if they persevere in the Christian life.

Tuesday: The Redemption of Creation (Rom 8:18-25)

The Lectionary continues its reading from Romans 8 without passing over any verses. Accordingly, homilists who are attentive to Paul's train of thought will notice the way in which he constructs and develops his instruction on the new life that believers enjoy in the Spirit.

Thus far Paul has reminded the Romans that they are no longer in the realm of the flesh but in the realm of God's Spirit because they dwell in Christ, the new Adam (Saturday's reading). Consequently, they are sons and daughters of God, coheirs with Christ, who will be glorified with Christ at the general resurrection of the dead if they suffer with him (Monday's reading). Having spoken of the glory that awaits those who persevere with Christ, in today's reading the Apostle speaks in terms of cosmic redemption. It is not only humankind that will be saved; it is the whole of creation that will be redeemed.

After encouraging the Romans to suffer with Christ in order to be glorified with him, Paul notes that there is no comparison between the sufferings of the present and the glory that will be revealed in those who believe in Christ. Next, Paul personifies creation, speaking of creation as if it were a living person. Not only are we waiting for the glory that is to be revealed in us, creation itself is waiting for the revelation of our glory. Why? Because when humankind sinned, creation was subjected to "futility." Consequently, creation could not attain its goal because humankind was not able to attain its goal: participation in God's glory. This is why creation itself is waiting for our glorification at the general resurrection of the dead, for when this happens, creation will finally attain its goal.

Paul, then, speaks of the "groaning" of creation as well as the "groaning" of the believer. Believers, who have already received the gift of the Spirit, are groaning for the redemption of their bodies, which will occur at the general resurrection of the dead. And creation is "groaning" (in the sense of sighing and longing) for its own redemption that will occur when this takes place.

At the end of this reading Paul says that believers have been saved in hope. This means that although we have *already* been justified and reconciled to God, we have *not yet* been finally saved. Final salvation will only occur when our bodies are redeemed at the general resurrection of the dead.

This is a marvelous reading that expands our understanding of what the New Testament means when it speaks of salvation. It is not only our soul that will be saved; it will be the whole of us that will be saved. It is not only we who will be saved; it is the whole of God's creation that will be saved.

Wednesday: The Groaning of the Spirit (Rom 8:26-30)

Today's reading consists of two subunits. In the first half of the reading (8:26-27) Paul continues the theme of "groaning" that he introduced in yesterday's lesson. In the second half of the reading (8:28-30) the Apostle speaks of God's divine plan or economy of our salvation.

Whereas yesterday we heard about the groaning of creation and our groaning for final redemption, today Paul speaks of the "inexpressible groanings" (8:26) of the Spirit, by which he means the way the Spirit intercedes on our behalf to God. Paul explains this groaning of the Spirit in terms of our weakness. Because we do not know how to pray as we ought to pray, the Spirit of God comes to our assistance. Thus, when Christians pray, they pray in the Spirit inasmuch as the Spirit assists them in their prayers and intercedes for them according to the will of God. The groaning of the Spirit, then, is not the longing of the Spirit for something but the Spirit's inexpressible sighs on our behalf.

Paul's remark about the will of God (8:28) leads to the second part of this reading in which the Apostle describes the economy of salvation. God foreknew us; God predestined us to be conformed to Christ; God called us; God justified us; and God will glorify us at the general resurrection of the dead. Nothing has been left to chance; those who are in Christ are part of a larger plan that will work for their good.

Those who preach from this text will do well to focus on either the first or the second part of this reading. If they choose the first part, they can instruct the congregation on the role that the Spirit plays in our prayer life. We do not pray alone. We pray in and through the power of God's Spirit that enables us to pray in a way that conforms to God's will. Those who preach from the second part of this reading should remind the congregation that all of us are part of a great economy of salvation. Nothing has been left to chance.

Thursday: Nothing to Fear (Rom 8:31b-39)

Today's reading brings to a close the Lectionary readings of Romans 8 that began on Saturday and have continued without interruption until today. This reading is the climax of the first eight chapters of the letter, and most congregations will have little difficulty in grasping its central message that nothing can separate us from God's love for us.

Paul begins by asking a series of rhetorical questions whose response should be self-evident. Who can stand against those whom God defends? If God gave his own Son in death, will not God give us everything else as well? If God has acquitted us, who will charge us? Who can condemn us?

Toward the end of this reading, Paul expresses his personal conviction that nothing can separate the justified from God's love for them that is experienced in Jesus Christ, who now reigns as their Lord. The entire passage is a tour de force intended to assure those whom God has justified and reconciled that nothing can separate them from God's love.

Those who choose to preach from this passage will do well to take one of Paul's rhetorical questions and develop it. For example, "If God is for us, who can be against us?" Such a question allows the homilist to remind the congregation of what they already know but too often forget because of the worries and anxieties of life. In light of all that God has done for us in his Son, the justified have no reason to let the worries and anxieties of their lives overwhelm them. All will be well because God's love in Christ is irrevocable.

Friday: Paul's Anguish for Israel (Rom 9:1-5)

For the next three days the Lectionary presents us with readings taken from Romans 9–11, a section in which Paul deals with Israel's failure to embrace the gospel. This question of Israel's failure to accept the gospel is of central importance for Paul because it raises the question of God's faithfulness to Israel. Have God's ways changed? Has God rejected Israel? The careful response that Paul gives to these questions in Romans 9–11 can be summarized in this way: It is not God who has been unfaithful to Israel; it is Israel that has been unfaithful to God. Seeking its own way of righteousness, Israel missed the way of righteousness that God manifested in the saving death and resurrection of Christ. Israel's failure, however, is not the final word. This failure, which is a temporary hardening of Israel, has resulted in God's mercy for the Gentiles. God has not rejected Israel, and Israel still remains God's people. In God's own time, in God's own way, Israel will be saved.

Today's reading summarizes Paul's grief and sorrow at the failure of the majority of his people to embrace the gospel. Paul goes so far as to say that he would be willing to be separated from Christ if his separation from the Lord would result in Israel believing in the gospel. The Apostle then enumerates the privileges of Israel, the last and most important of which is "the Christ," the Messiah. These privileges remain the privileges of Israel; they have not been revoked or taken away.

The readings from Romans 9–11 are an opportunity to remind the congregation of the central role that the Jewish people continue to play in the economy of salvation. In preaching today's text homilists will want to emphasize Paul's love for his people. Because the Jewish people remain God's people, there is no place for anti-Semitism in Christianity. Like Paul, those who are in Christ continue to pray for the good and the welfare of God's chosen people from whom the Messiah came forth.

Saturday: God Has Not Rejected Israel
(Rom 11:1-2a, 11-12, 25-29)

Skipping over most of chapter 9 and all of chapter 10, today's reading presents us with highlights from Romans 11. If preachers hope to comprehend what Paul is saying in this chapter, they must read it in the context of Romans 9–11. The manner in which the Lectionary structures this material highlights three points: (1) God has not rejected Israel; (2) Israel has stumbled, but it has not fallen; (3) Israel will be saved.

Paul begins with the most crucial question: "Has God rejected his people?" (11:1). The answer one gives is of central importance because if God has rejected Israel, then God has been unfaithful to his people, and there is no reason to trust in God today. But Paul is emphatic that this is not the case. There is a remnant of Israel that has believed, and Paul belongs to that remnant. Accordingly, just as God left a remnant during the days of Elijah, so God has left a remnant at the present time.

Next, Paul asks if Israel has stumbled so as to fall. Once more the answer is negative. Israel has stumbled over the Messiah inasmuch as it has been scandalized by the way that God manifested saving righteousness in the crucified Messiah. But this is not the end of the story. Israel's failure has led to salvation for the Gentiles. But if this is the result of Israel's failure, imagine what will happen when Israel embraces the gospel.

Finally, lest the Gentile Christians at Rome become self-confident and denigrate unbelieving Israel, Paul reveals a mystery. A certain hardening has come over Israel at the present time until the full number of the Gentiles embraces the faith. When this happens, all Israel will be saved.

This is an important reading for the congregation to hear and for homilists to proclaim. Preachers will do well to focus on Paul's strong affirmation that God has not rejected the Jewish people. The Jewish people remain God's people, and in God's time and way they will experience God's final salvation.

Monday: God's Mercy and Wisdom (Rom 11:29-36)

Today's reading, which consists of two units, brings Paul's discussion of Israel to a close. In the first unit (11:29-32) Paul reminds the Roman Christians (most of whom appear to have been Gentiles) of the mercy that God has extended to them, and which God will extend to Israel. In the second (11:33-36), Paul marvels as he contemplates the wisdom and knowledge of God's economy of salvation for Gentile and Jew alike.

In the first part of the reading the focus is on God's mercy in the face of human disobedience. Once the Gentiles disobeyed God, but now, because of Israel's disobedience, they have received God's mercy. But this is not the end of God's economy of salvation. Just as Israel's disobedience led to mercy for the Gentiles, the mercy that God has extended to the Gentiles will lead to mercy for Israel. As Paul understands the divine economy, God delivered both the Jewish people and the Gentiles to disobedience for the expressed purpose of extending mercy to both. This is why Paul proclaims that God's gifts and Israel's election (which Paul described in last Friday's reading) are irrevocable. God's mercy, not human disobedience, is the final word. It is the only word that counts.

In the second part of this reading Paul expresses his wonder and amazement at the way in which God has structured the divine economy of salvation. Although humans can know something of God, they will never be able to comprehend the riches of God's wisdom and knowledge. Who would have thought that God would manifest his saving righteousness by the death of his Son on the cross? Who would have thought that God would find a way to extend mercy to Gentiles and Jews in the face of so much human disobedience?

A homily on this reading will do best to focus on either the first or the second part of the lesson. Homilists who focus on the first part of the reading might highlight the paradoxical way in which God's mercy manifests itself, for despite human disobedience, God finds a way to extend mercy to all. Those who focus on the second part of the reading might emphasize our need to stand in wonder and awe before the mystery of God whose ways and judgments will always be beyond human understanding.

Tuesday: Life within the Body of Christ (Rom 12:5-16ab)

This is the first of three readings drawn from the fifth part of Romans (12:1–15:13), which I have titled "God's Righteousness and the Moral Life of the Justified." In this part of the letter Paul explains the ethical implications of the gospel he proclaims. Those who have been justified on the basis of trusting faith in what God has done in Jesus Christ will live morally good lives that reflect their new relationship to God. In the fifth and final part of Romans Paul describes what this new life entails.

Today's reading presents two aspects of this morally good life: living as members of the Body of Christ and practicing a love that is genuine and sincere.

The first part of the reading (12:5-8) deals with living the morally good life within the Body of Christ. Here, Paul reminds the Romans that they are related to each other in a startling new way because each of them has been incorporated into Christ's body by baptism into his death. Moreover, as members of Christ's body, each of them has received a gift for the good of the whole body. Consequently, their new life in Christ summons them to exercise their gifts in ways that will benefit the entire body.

The second part of the reading (12:9-16ab) begins with an exhortation that establishes the theme for everything that follows: "Let love be sincere." The implication of this statement is that it is possible to practice a kind of love that is insincere and hypocritical. The material that follows illustrates what Paul means by sincere love. Toward the end of this reading, he exhorts the Romans not to retaliate against their enemies. Instead, they should bless their persecutors. What he writes here is reminiscent of Jesus' exhortation of non-retaliation in the Sermon on the Mount (Matt 5:44).

This reading is, for the most part, self-explanatory. Consequently, it will be immediately accessible to most congregations. Instead of simply repeating these injunctions, then, a homily on this text might emphasize the connection between the gospel of

God's saving righteousness and the morally good life that believers are called to live. The moral life is not a series of burdensome rules and commands but the outcome of the new life believers enjoy in Christ. Such a life expresses itself in sincere love within the Body of Christ.

Wednesday: How the Law Is Fulfilled (Rom 13:8-10)

Throughout his letter to the Romans Paul has insisted that people are not justified—put in a right relation with God—on the basis of doing the works of the Mosaic Law but on the basis of God's gracious act in Jesus Christ in which they must believe with trusting faith. Thus salvation is not the outcome of something human beings do but of something God does for them.

Paul's teaching on justification, however, has been a stumbling block for many. If this is the case, how are the justified to live morally good lives? Is Paul saying that we can disobey God's law as long as we believe in God? Paul's curt response to this objection would be, "of course not!"

In today's reading the Apostle explains that the justified fulfill the law by the love commandment. Quoting four commandments from the Decalogue, he writes that all the commandments are "summed up" in the love commandment. He then concludes that the love commandment fulfills the law. To appreciate what Paul says here, it is important to understand his concept of love. The kind of love that Paul has in view is the love that Christ manifested for us when he died for our sins. The quality of love that Paul has in view is sincere and without hypocrisy; it is the kind of love described in yesterday's reading. The love that Paul has in view blesses the enemy and refuses to retaliate. Love in this way, Paul says, and you will fulfill all God's commandments. Sincere love does not violate the commandments of the Decalogue.

Preaching from this text offers homilists an opportunity to explain the relationship between law and love in Paul's teaching on justification by faith and to clarify the Pauline meaning of love. Although the justified are no longer "under the law," they fulfill the law by loving each other and their enemies in the way that Christ loved and died for them.

Thursday: On Not Judging Others (Rom 14:7-12)

Today's reading is part of a larger section in which Paul deals with a specific situation within the Roman church (14:1–15:13). The problem can be summarized in this way: Like most congregations, the church at Rome was composed of different factions that viewed the Christian life differently. In the case of the Roman congregation, there were some who continued to observe the Jewish holy days and dietary prescriptions of the Mosaic Law. Paul identifies this faction as "the weak" because of their delicate conscience. Other believers, whom Paul calls "the strong" because of their robust conscience, no longer followed these prescriptions of the law. The problem was that these groups were judging and condemning each other. Consequently, both factions were threatening the unity of the church.

Although Paul tended to side with the strong, he did not take up their cause. Instead, he sought to bring both sides together for the sake of the church's unity. The weak should not judge the strong, and the strong should be willing to curb some of their freedom for the sake of the weak.

In today's reading Paul presents both factions with a powerful argument for moderating their positions. Those who are in Christ no longer live for themselves; they live for Christ who died for them. Consequently, whether they live or die, they belong to the Lord. Given this new relationship to Christ, it is utterly incomprehensible why a Christian would judge another Christian, since all will be judged by God.

The background I have summarized is more important for the homilist than for the congregation. Given the limited time there is to preach at the daily liturgy, the homilist may want to focus on the believer's new relationship to Christ and the coming final judgment that should discourage the justified from judging each other. Since all of Christ's faithful are servants of the same Lord, and since all will be judged by the same God, there is no need to judge each other.

Friday: Paul's Priestly Service for the Gospel (Rom 15:14-21)

Today's reading comes from the closing of the letter to the Romans (15:14–16:27). Paul does several things in the closing.

He (1) reminds the Romans of the apostolic commission he has received to preach the gospel among the Gentiles; (2) explains his plans to visit Jerusalem, Rome, and then go on to Spain; (3) greets a number of the Roman Christians by name; and (4) sends greetings to the Romans from Corinth, from where he writes this letter. The focus of today's reading is the first part of the letter closing: Paul's apostolic commission to preach the gospel to the Gentiles.

In describing his apostolic commission Paul makes three points. First, he employs the language of Israel's cult to describe his ministry among the Gentiles. Although he was not a priest and could not be a priest since he did not belong to the tribe of Levi, Paul portrays his apostolate as a "priestly service" whereby he offers to God the gift of the Gentiles he has gained for the gospel. Second, Paul insists that he boasts only in what God had accomplished in him. His ministry has been powerful and effective because God has been at work in him. Third, he says that he has always striven to preach Christ where Christ has not yet been preached rather than to build on another's foundation.

Since we are coming to the end of the Lectionary readings on Romans, a homily on today's reading would do well to remind the congregation of the man who wrote the letter to which we have been listening. To do this the homilist might focus on all or any one of the three points noted above: (1) the priestly nature of Paul's ministry, (2) the power of God that was at work in Paul's ministry, (3) the missionary dimension of Paul's ministry that led him to preach Christ to those who had not yet heard of Christ.

Saturday: The Obedience of Faith (Rom 16:3-9, 16, 22-27)

With today's reading the Lectionary concludes its semi-continuous reading of Romans. The reading has three parts: (1) Paul's greetings to specific Christians at Rome, (2) greetings from those with Paul to those at Rome, (3) a final benediction.

The Lectionary gives only a partial list of the people that Paul greets at Rome. But the list is sufficient to show that even though he has never visited the city, he knows several people there. This wide circle of acquaintances at Rome would have kept Paul informed about what was happening to the church there. In greeting so many people by name Paul establishes a rapport with those who did not know him but had heard rumors about him and the gospel he preached.

After greeting people at Rome Paul extends greetings to the Romans from those who are with him. Note that Paul is staying in the house of Gaius, a Corinthian whom he baptized, according to 1 Cor 1:14. This suggests that Paul wrote this letter from Corinth, sometime during the mid-fifties. Tertius, the scribe who wrote this letter (which Paul dictated) also sends his greetings. Dictating the letter to Tertius would have allowed Paul an opportunity to test phrases out loud for rhetorical effect before Tertius wrote them.

Finally, Paul concludes with a benediction that speaks of the gospel that has been kept secret for ages but has now been revealed in order to bring about "the obedience of faith" to all the nations. This phrase, "the obedience of faith," is the same phrase that Paul used at the beginning of the letter (Monday of the twenty-eighth week). It is Paul's way of summarizing what faith in the gospel entails: complete and utter obedience to God in Jesus Christ, through the power of God's Spirit.

A homily on this text might focus on "the obedience of faith." In doing so it would remind the congregation that we are ending our reading of Romans where we began it: with a summons to the obedience that faith requires. From start to finish this letter has been about the faith that is perfect obedience to God.

Resources for Preaching from Romans

Achtemeier, Paul J. *Romans*. Interpretation: A Bible Commentary for Teaching and Preaching. Louisville: Westminster John Knox Press, 1985. (Written specifically for preachers, this commentary is a good resource for preaching from this letter.)

Barrett, C. K. *A Commentary on the Epistle to the Romans*. Harper's New Testament Commentaries. New York: Harper & Row, 1957. (Although older, this is a brief and succinct commentary that has been reprinted by Hendrickson Press.)

Bray, Gerald, ed. *Romans*. Ancient Christian Commentary on Scripture. New Testament 6. Downers Grove: InterVarsity Press, 1998. (This volume provides a series of quotations from Patristic commentaries on Romans.)

Byrne, Brendan. *Romans*. Sacra Pagina 6. Collegeville: Liturgical Press, 1996. (This commentary by a Roman Catholic scholar provides a rich theological reading of the text.)

Cranfield, C. E. B. *Romans: A Shorter Commentary*. Grand Rapids: Eerdmans, 1985. (This is a distillation of Cranfield's magisterial two-volume commentary on Romans.)

Fitzmyer, Joseph A. *Romans: A New Translation with Introduction and Commentary*. The Anchor Bible 33. New York: Doubleday, 1993. (A commentary on Romans from one of the most important Roman Catholic scholars of the past century. This commentary is now being published by Yale University Press.)

Grieb, Katherine A. *The Story of Romans: A Narrative Defense of God's Righteousness*. Louisville: Westminster John Knox Press, 2002. (This brief but rich book provides readers with an excellent introduction to reading Romans as a narrative.)

Keck, Leander. *Romans*. Abingdon New Testament Commentaries. Nashville: Abingdon Press, 2005. (This is a brief but insightful commentary that is rich in theological exposition.)

Matera, Frank J. *Romans*. Paideia. Grand Rapids: Baker Academic, 2010. (My commentary is intended for students at the M. A. level. In addition to tracing the train of thought for each unit of the letter, it deals with the theological issues the letter raises.)

Wright, N. T. *The Letter to the Romans*. The New Interpreter's Bible: A Commentary in Twelve Volumes. Volume 10. Nashville: Abingdon Press, 2002. (This commentary is part of a larger series for preachers. Wright's commentary is an insightful and theologically rewarding reading of Romans.)